THE BEATLES AND FASHION

FAB GEAR

The Love of My Life

Paolo Hewitt

THE BEATLES AND FASHION
FAB GEAR

PRESTEL
MUNICH · LONDON · NEW YORK

ADVENTURES IN PEPPERLAND

Page 112

STRAWBERRY TEDDY BOYS FOREVER

Page 6

3

IT'S ONLY BEATLEMANIA

Page 40

CONTENTS

HUR, THERE AND EVERYWHERE
Page 158

THE LITTLE SHOP ON THE CORNER
Page 192

FAB THANKS AND PICTURE CREDITS
Page 236

REFERENCES
Page 237

INDEX
Page 238

GRETSCH

STRAWBERRY TEDDY BOYS FOREVER
Chapter One

There was no point asking if they really got on together. It's obvious they do. When one makes a joke, the others roar with laughter. They have their own 'inside' language when they want to keep something private. … And they've been together so much, sometimes they don't even have to talk in code. As Paul says, 'We can just read each other's thought waves.'

STEVE BRANDT · PHOTOPLAY MAGAZINE · 1964

Their *clothes*? Yes, their clothes, because not only are clothes deeply entwined with Beatle history but because clothes are important, highly important. And I am not the only one to think so. 'More than any other area of taste,' according to the great writer Nik Cohn, 'they are statements – complex expressions of self-image, of how one sees oneself and what one hopes for. However one dresses, it carries one's own dream of oneself, and this applies just as much to dowdiness as to peacockery.'

Research and the memories of others show us that The Beatles used clothes for many reasons – for disguise, for humour, for criminal activity. They used clothes to shock, and they used clothes pragmatically. They used clothes to express solidarity and, conversely, to display the band's hierarchy. They popularised certain items, but above all they used clothes to differentiate themselves from all their contemporaries.

From an early age The Beatles had a keen sense of themselves as something far more than a pop band. They were a force for change, and they knew it. Clothes were a way of pushing forward that change, of acknowledging the trailblazing path they were on. As John Lennon once remarked: 'To a degree we can make a trend popular – we don't usually invent clothes, we wear something we like and then maybe people follow us. … We changed the hairstyles and the clothes of the world, including America. They were a very square and sorry lot when we went over.'

The Beatles adored clothes; they were a major part of the group's DNA. They grew up in a time when looking smart both on and off stage was paramount. That is why you rarely see a photo of the band looking scruffy or untogether. Image was vital, whether it be to shake a young girl's heart or to impress the pop underground. Clothes also helped to bond The Beatles, allowing them to be presented to the world as a striking entity.

'Mick Jagger called us the Four-Headed Monster because we went everywhere together, dressed similarly', Paul McCartney once said. 'We'd all have black polo-neck sweaters and dark suits and the same haircut, so we did look like a four-headed monster.'

OPPOSITE George Harrison in the Star Club, Hamburg, in 1962, playing up to the camera. For many, George would remain the best-dressed Beatle.

According to Ringo: 'We'd all go to the same shop. I'd get the shirt in blue, and someone would get it in pink, and someone would get it in button-down. If you look at all the photos, we are all dressed in the same style because that's how it happened. … We were going to all these shops and buying little uniforms for ourselves. That's also why we looked like Beatles: beside the haircut, we were all looking the same.'

Clothes allowed The Beatles to change the world of entertainment for ever. As the first authorised Beatle biographer, Billy Shepherd (in fact, journalist Peter Jones), informs us in his book *The True Story of The Beatles*, 'Groups wore grey suits, with matching ties and clean polished shoes. Everything was neat, tidy, restrained and totally lacking in originality. There was only one Shadows group, but there were hundreds all over the country trying to make the same noise and create the same picture.'

The Beatles changed all that. If they were going to wear suits, they would wear suits their way. If they were going to have their hair shaped (hair is dealt with in Chapter Four), they would have it styled their way. The Beatles were the now and the future, and there was an honesty about their stance which many found utterly refreshing.

'The Beatles', cooed the magazine *Fab 208* in early 1964, 'mock all the old traditions and trappings of stardom. They insist on being themselves. Natural. Honest. No Lies. No pretence. And no baloney.'

Clothes played a huge part in that process. The Beatles subverted the suit, sent sales of polo-neck sweaters soaring, launched the Beatle boot and then, when they gave up touring, they took that which was hip – the Dandy, the Hippie – and made it popular. Just as their music bought together disparate sources and welded them into a refreshing and forward-thinking sound, so their clothes acted in precisely the same way.

Timing was, of course, important. For example, The Beatles could not have succeeded in America in such a spectacular fashion had it not been for the terrible assassination of John F. Kennedy in November 1963. America in the mid-'60s was in desperate need of something new and bright and positive to counteract the great surge of worry and despair that had swept through the country after the President's shocking murder. In their dress and in the upbeat character they continually pushed at the American public, The Beatles fulfilled that particular need completely. And Lady Luck was also on their side in terms of their physical appearance. The Beatles fitted together perfectly: not a blonde amongst them. As the author and DJ Spencer Leigh points out: 'You see the Kinks in those hunting jackets and you think, you look wrong. But whatever The Beatles wore, even the silliest costumes, they looked fine. It was incredible.'

Liverpool, of course, helped shape their fashion instincts. The Beatles grew up in a city devastated by the Second World War. The town lost 4,000 citizens and 6,585 homes to German bombs. But by the time The Beatles reached their teenage years, Liverpool was on the mend. Manufacturing and the famous Liverpool port were attracting money into the city. Ships regularly sailed for New York, and the demand of visiting or returning sailors for entertainment accounted for the huge amount of clubs and live bands in the city.

Clothes-wise, the New York connection meant that Liverpool was far ahead of many UK cities. Young seamen known as 'Cunard Yanks' (after the Cunard shipping line) would bring back stacks of American shirts, ties and suits, as well as jeans, a fashion item hard to access anywhere else in the country. The British sailors would sport the latest American look in the Liverpool pubs and draw all the admiring glances.

'You could always tell the sailors, they were the best-dressed', Ringo Starr once noted. Billy Hatton, of the Liverpool band The Fourmost (contemporaries of The Beatles), concurs. 'Those sailors brought American fashions back to us', he tells me over a mid-afternoon drink. 'You could always tell in a local pub when some of the boats had come back, because you would see these really smartly dressed fellas in the pub. We all wanted to dress like them.'

Hatton is an interesting guide to the Liverpool of the 1950s. He grew up in the Dingle, the same rough area that Ringo Starr was raised in, and he remembers the late '40s and early '50s as a time of gloomy conformity. 'All the lads looked like their dads, and all the girls looked like their mums', he recalls. 'There was a lot of passing down of clothes. Because there were not any fatties in those days – big lack of food, you see – a lot of the clothes that the dads handed down fitted quite well. When the young people got their independence – maybe not financially but spiritually, socially – they wanted to be different. There was plenty of work in those days, loads of part-time jobs, so the young could get some money together. This is the mid-'50s, and that is when the Teddy Boys came along in their Edwardian dress.'

Let us tread carefully here. While Hatton's memories are not to be contested, others were on a different path. The Beatles' first tailor, Walter Smith, who we will meet very soon, was an early Modernist, dressing sharply and listening to big band jazz every Monday night. Walter did not take to the first post-Second World War youth-quake, the Teddy Boys. Too crude, too garish for Walter's tastes, I would imagine. Yet the effect was highly important. The Teddy Boys were true pioneers, working-class boys adopting an upper-class look to create a national fashion. Before the Second World War, fashion was invented at the top and then drifted down to the masses. The Teddy Boys changed all that and started the necessary process of separating the young from the old. From the Teddy Boys onwards, urban streets would set the pace, not the moneyed classes.

The Teddy Boy style originated in London in 1954 and reached Liverpool in 1956. It was an outlandish style. The coats were Edwardian, with black velvet collars (a touch that The Beatles would later use in their early stage suits); shirts were worn with bootlace ties, and coloured suits – powder blue, for example – were given the thumbs up.

In the early '50s men's trousers were baggy, loose-fitting. 'You could make a sail out of them', Hatton jokes. But the Teddy Boys opted for tight-fitting trousers with no flare whatsoever. They were called drainpipe trousers, known in Liverpool as 'drainies'. As soon as they became popular, scores of Liverpool teenagers headed to the tailors to have their twenty-inch-bottom trousers narrowed to fourteen inches or much less.

OPPOSITE A Teddy Boy caught on camera in 1955. The Beatles would appropriate the drape jacket's velvet collar at a later date.

Drainies were worn with green fluorescent socks and big, clumpy shoes, be they brogues or brothel creepers. The Teddy Boy hairstyle finished off the look in dramatic style.

'The hair was done different', Hatton explains. 'You had the quiff at the front, and then the hair was combed straight around the back of the ears and then a parting at the back which was called a DA ['duck's arse'].'

In this manner the Teddy Boys broke for ever the clothing link between father and son. Pete Shotton was John Lennon's closest and longest-lasting friend. He went to school with John, where they fought and then bonded. He remembers the Teddy Boys very well. 'Prior to their emergence,' he once wrote, 'we'd never questioned our parents' inherent right to dictate our choice of clothing. "If it's good enough for your dad, it's good enough for you."' For the young, good enough was not good enough any more.

The Teddy Boy style defied normality, challenged all rules. That made John Winston Lennon a Teddy Boy waiting to happen.

Born on 9 October 1940, by his teenage years Lennon was a hurting soul. He saw his father, Freddy, and his mother, Julia, walk away from him at an early age. He was raised by his aunt Mimi, and he would not see his father again until he was a national celebrity. His father's place was taken by Mimi's husband, George Smith. The boy drew close to Smith, but when Lennon was fourteen, Smith succumbed to cancer. Two years later his mother, whom in later years he had grown close to – she had taught him the banjo and bought him a guitar – was killed in a road accident.

In effect, he had lost his mother and father twice. When the Teddy Boy look hit Liverpool, Lennon instinctively responded to its delinquent clarion call.

Teddy Boys were against the adult world, and as far as John was concerned, the adult world had done little except let him down.

Paul McCartney backs this assertion up. 'It was this tragedy [John's mother dying] that led John to be a wild guy, a Ted. There was a lot of aggression in Liverpool; there were lots of Teddy Boys and you had to try and avoid them if you saw them in alleyways. If, like John, you were a guy who lived on his own, you had to put up some kind of a front. So he grew long sideburns, he had a long drape jacket, he had the drainpipe trousers and the crepe-soled shoes. He was always quite defensive because of that; I would see him from afar, from the bus. This Ted would get on the bus and I wouldn't look at him too hard in case he hit me.'

Lennon channelled his bubbling aggression into the attitude his clothing demanded. 'Strike before they strike you' became his major defence mechanism. His tongue was made sharp, his presence in public made threatening. 'John's attitude was to fight insecurities, hence the aggression that came out in different ways', Cynthia Lennon, his first wife, noted. 'He would never allow people to see his insecurities.'

Although his style and demeanour made him a feared force in local circles (Paul McCartney was very wary of John before they met), in truth Lennon was nowhere near the real deal. The real Teddy Boys in Liverpool were not only older than John but also highly dangerous people. Many of them carried knives, iron bars, even meat cleavers, and were never afraid to use these fearsome weapons. A Liverpool Teddy Boy, Lennon soon realised, was something to be feared.

'I used to dress tough like a Teddy Boy, but if I went into tough districts and came across other Teddy Boys I was in danger', Lennon would later say. 'Liverpool's quite a tough city. A lot of the real Teddy Boys were actually in their early twenties. They were dockers. We were only fifteen, we were kids – they had hatchets, belts, bicycle chains and real weapons. We never really got into that.'

Tony Bramwell, a Liverpool contemporary who would work with the band for ten years, confirms John was a Weekend Ted, ironically the kind of character Lennon would write about in coded form in his song 'Day Tripper'. 'The Teds did not take kindly to people they thought were mimicking them', Bramwell told me. 'They took themselves very seriously.'

In 1957, after failing all his school exams, John was accepted into Liverpool College of Art. At that time Liverpool's art students dressed in a Beatnik style. They put on duffel coats, scarves, corduroy trousers and ill-fitting polo-neck sweaters, and made sure a copy of Jack Kerouac's book *On the Road* was stuffed inside a pocket. The look was down, dowdy, scruffy, a reaction against the mainstream suit-and-

LEFT Paul and John as The Quarrymen, opening the Casbah Club on 29 August 1959. John's future wife, Cynthia, is the girl smiling at Paul.

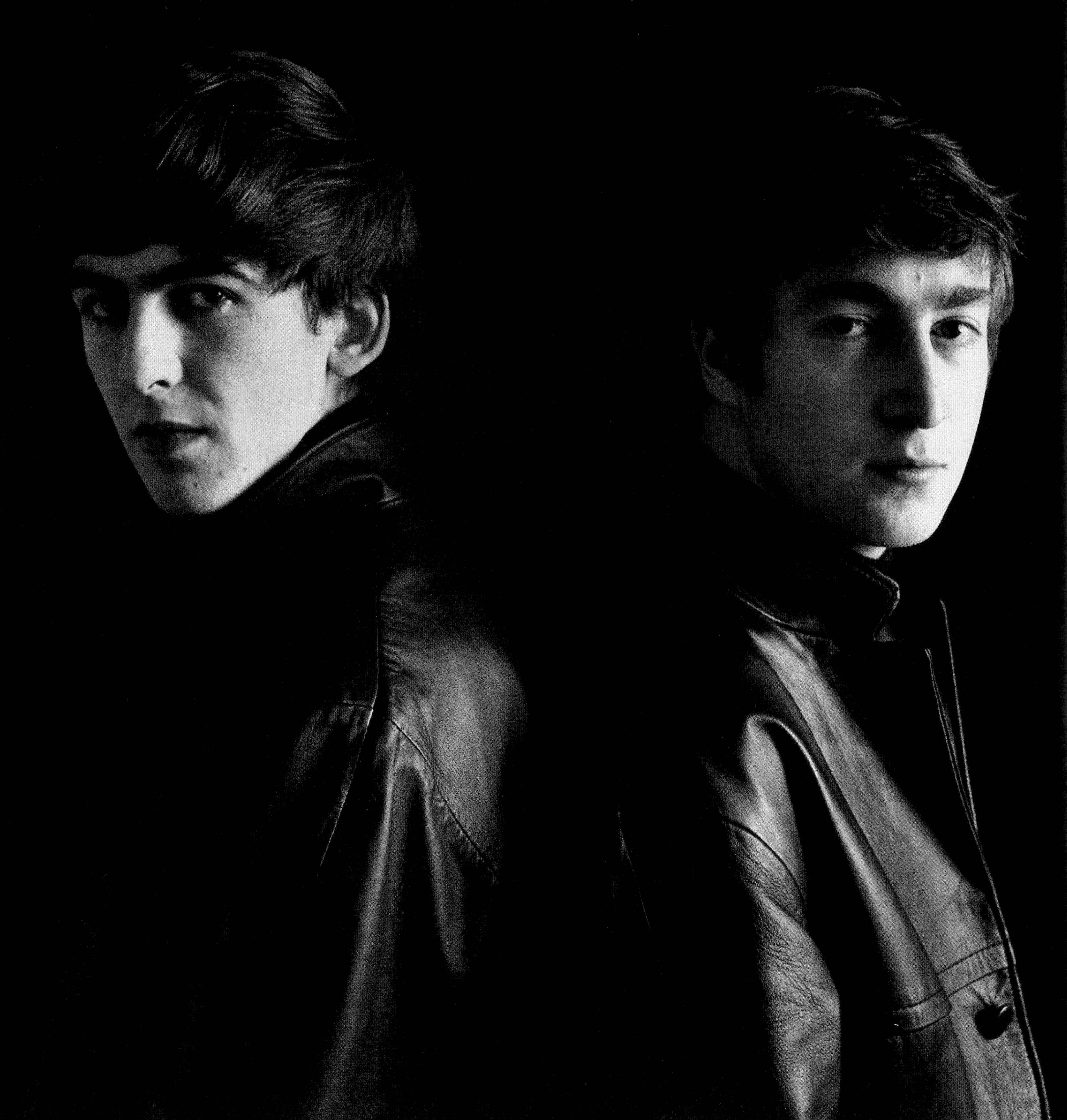

OPPOSITE George Harrison and John Lennon pose in leather for Astrid Kirchherr's camera. Their use of leather was inspired by Kirchherr and her friends Jürgen Vollmer and Klaus Voormann, and made the band one of the most radical-looking groups in Britain.

ABOVE A German Teddy Boy poses in a Hamburg street, April 1961.

RIGHT The famous rocker Gene Vincent posing in 1960. His appearance on British TV in 1959, dressed all in leather, consolidated the image of the rocker as wild boy.

FAR RIGHT The Teddy Boy craze gave birth to many different offshoots. Along with the rockers there were the Ton-Up Boys, so named because of their powerful motor bikes. They dressed all in leather, just like The Beatles.

tie look that dominated the Liverpool streets they walked. The Beatnik look said, 'I'm a drop-out, don't bother me.' It was sour, but it was never aggressive.

Lennon now jumped on the chance to use his Teddy Boy clothes for two distinct purposes: to separate himself from the herd and to provoke his classmates. Remember: strike before they strike you.

Bill Harry, later to become editor of the Liverpool publication *Mersey Beat*, was a college friend of Lennon's. 'The first time I noticed John Lennon,' Harry says, 'was when he stalked into the canteen with a group of friends. He stuck out like a sore thumb. At the college, as in various groups or communities, large or small, people tended to dress alike. The unconventional differing from the conventional and ending up looking, acting, thinking and dressing in the same way. John was different. Everyone else wore the type of gear students tended to wear at the end of the '50s: chunky sweaters, tight trousers, duffel coats in shades of fawn, black or navy blue. John was a Ted. There he was stalking about the canteen; tall, skinny with a DA haircut, drainies, heavily rimmed glasses and a Teddy Boy drape jacket. A bit of a weirdo, I thought.'

In this way Lennon's Teddy Boy style gave him what all pop stars crave – mass attention.

A Teddy Boy he may have been, but at the same time a certain confusion was starting to infiltrate Lennon's idea of himself. Often he found himself being torn, as he himself tells us, 'between being a Teddy Boy or an art student. One week I'd go to art school with my art school scarf on and my hair down and the next week I'd go for the leather jacket and the tight jeans ...'

Thug or artist? Artist or thug? As Lennon stood in front of his wardrobe and wrestled with his opposing instincts, the drummer Ringo Starr was another experiencing the massive effect of the Teddy Boy phenomenon.

Born Richard Starkey on 9 July 1940, Ringo was raised in the tough working-class area of Liverpool known as the Dingle. The simmering violence around him taught him an early life lesson – use clothes pragmatically. As soon as he was old enough, Ringo became a Teddy Boy. If he hadn't, he would have had the living daylights knocked out of him every time he ventured on to the street.

'The choices were,' Ringo once revealed, 'you could either be beaten up by anybody in your neighbourhood or by people in other neighbourhoods.'

Ringo's earliest Teddy Boy clothing was given to him by a sailor cousin. ('It all revolves around sailors', he once remarked.) Later, when he began work, he would buy his own Teddy Boy gear and beg, borrow and barter the other items. His was the Dingle gang, and there was a lot of a hanging around on street corners, playing the peacock to the girls, playing the tough man to the boys, waiting for the world to happen. Eventually, Ringo reversed this process – he went out and made the world happen around him.

The Teddy Boy craze generally passed Paul McCartney by, for reasons we will come to in a minute. George Harrison also differed. In fact, George's early attitude to clothes mirrored his role in The Beatles. From an early age George made adjustments to his clothes on a regular basis; in later life he went on to make adjustments to Lennon and McCartney's music. George's forte would be to take something good and make it even better.

As Billy Shepherd writes, 'George at school was something to behold. He decided that clothes did make the man and proceeded to adapt the school uniform to such an extent that he had frequent brushes with authority. He would wear with the deceivingly casual air of a Beau Brummell specially tight Harrison trousers and suede shoes. Not to mention multicoloured waistcoats. ... He hated the idea of being just one of a crowd, even if some people thought he looked like a "perishing actor" or something.'

Pete Shotton recalls George's luminous pink shirts, yellow waistcoats and drainpipe trousers. If this memory is correct, the wearing of such bright colours was both groundbreaking and highly courageous. The London stylist Carlo Manzi once recalled his mother dying his pink shirt white because she didn't want him to be thought gay. John Stephen, the man who made Carnaby Street, said that his ambition in life was to see a young man walk down the street in a pink shirt and not be called gay. The Small Faces' singer, Steve Marriott, was once chased down the

OPPOSITE In Hamburg one night George wore his hair combed forward. The disapproving looks he received from the crowd forced him back into the style shown in this shot from 1961.

street for wearing a pair of white trousers. Certain colours on men were deemed unwearable unless you wanted trouble of some kind.

In a hard-edged town such as Liverpool, full of dockers and other no-nonsense people, a pink shirt would, at the very least, draw negative attention. George seems to have cared little for the opinions of others. He eagerly took to fashion and to this day is regarded by many as the band's best dresser.

As a teenager he developed many ideas on the subject. *Beatles Monthly* once revealed that corduroy was one of George's favourite fabrics and that as a young man he approached a few cobblers to investigate the idea of creating a corduroy shoe.

'I started to develop my version of the school uniform', he once recalled. 'I had some cast-offs from my brother. One was a dog-toothed check-patterned sports coat, which I had dyed black to use as my school blazer. The colour hadn't quite taken, so it still had a slight check design to it. I had a shirt I bought in Lime Street that I thought was so cool. It was white with pleats down the front and it had black embroidery along the corner of the pleats.'

Born on 25 February 1943, by the time he had adapted the Teddy Boy style Harrison had met and befriended John Lennon. George was considerably younger than John. Clothes allowed Lennon to play the elder brother role to Harrison, the budding songwriter donating various items not long into their friendship.

'I had a waistcoat John had given me, which he'd got from his uncle Dykins [his mother's boyfriend]', George recalled. 'It was like an evening suit waistcoat, black, double-breasted with lapels. The trousers John also gave me soon after we first met – powder-blue drainpipes with turn-ups. I dyed them black as well. And I had black suede shoes from my brother. Aunt Mimi's husband was George Smith and his brother was our English teacher at the Institute. ... He was always saying, "They are not school shoes, Harrison. Come and stand in Chewers Corner."'

'That outfit of mine was very risky and it felt like all day, every day, I was going to get busted. In those days we used Vaseline on our hair to get the rock 'n' roll greased-back hairstyle. Also you were supposed to wear a cap and a tie and a badge on your blazer. I didn't have my badge stitched on, I had it loose. It was held in place by a pen clipped over it in my top pocket, so I could remove it easily and the tie.'

OPPOSITE Paul with his famous Höfner bass guitar and all-leather look, taken at the Cavern Club, Liverpool, in 1960. Paul was now able to dress in a rebellious style and not worry his father too much.

George's parents were very understanding of their boy. But when they came home one night to find him wearing the jeans John had given him, they were shocked. For George's father, Harold, for whom baggy trousers were a sign of conformity and respectability, these jeans were just too much. 'Harold went spare,' recalled Mrs Harrison. 'When he saw them, he went over the moon. ... Then he [George] jumped up and pranced around the room. "How can I do my ballet without my tight jeans?" he said, dancing all over the place. We had to laugh at him in the end. George never gave us any cheek, but he always got round us.'

It was hard for the generation that had somehow survived the Second World War even to begin to understand the Teddy Boys. Not only was it a startling look but their exploits – rioting in dance halls and cinemas – horrified many. Beatle relatives were no different, as George Harrison was to discover.

'I remember going to John's house once soon after we met', he recalled. 'I was still at the Institute and I looked a bit young. We were trying to look like Teddy Boys – and I must have looked pretty good because Mimi did not like me at all. She was really shocked and said, "Look at him, why have you brought this boy round to my house? He looks dreadful, like a Teddy Boy."'

In fact, Aunt Mimi presented something of a problem for John when it came to Teddy Boy clothing. As she told the second official Beatles biographer, Hunter Davies: 'Up till John was sixteen, I always made sure he wore his regulation school blazer and shirt.'

Cynthia Lennon claims John would leave the house hiding his drainies under a pair of baggy trousers so as to escape Mimi's censure. And Hunter Davies confirms this trick. 'His way of getting them past Mimi was to put on old conventional trousers over his jeans, then take them off at the bus stop when he had got safely away from the house', he writes. Or he might, like the local singer Billy Fury, leave his clothes at a friend's house and change there.

Lennon was able to develop his look in teenage years because he was now seeing a lot more of his birth mother, Julia, and she would often give him extra pocket money, which would then go towards his clothing, allowing him to stay a step ahead of the pack – which was just how he liked it.

As Pete Shotton recalls, 'John, thanks in part to Julia's largesse, was the first to sport coloured shirts, thin ties, raincoats with padded shoulders and tight black jeans.'

One parent who thoroughly disapproved of John's look was Jim McCartney, father of James Paul McCartney, who was born on 18 June 1942. When he met Lennon at the Woolton village fête on 6 June 1957, Macca was very taken by a song called 'A White Sports Coat (And A Pink Carnation)', written by Marty Robbins and performed by the King Brothers.

In honour of that record, McCartney had acquired a white jacket, which he then matched against his dark trousers. Barry Miles describes him in his biography *Paul McCartney: Many Years From Now*: 'His white jacket had metallic threads which made the fabric sparkle, With it he wore very tight drainpipe trousers. It was a far remove from the school uniform which, like most teenage boys, Paul was obliged to wear most of the time. That consisted of grey trousers which he took to a tailor to have narrowed as much as he could get away with without his father complaining, a school tie and a blazer which he had also had skilfully altered.'

Paul's parents, Jim and Mary, had instilled in him the need to look smart and presentable every time you left the house. Your appearance reflected your family. Therefore it was imperative that in public you looked clean and neat at all times.

Tragically, Mary McCartney passed away from breast cancer when her son Paul was just eleven. Paul was very sensitive to the challenge facing his father, left to rear his sons alone. When the Teddy Boy craze hit Liverpool, Jim placed himself firmly against this youth cult. 'In his mind,' says Mark Lewisohn, the world's leading Beatle expert, 'Teddy Boys were delinquents, and in those days delinquents were the worst kind of people. Paul didn't want to put any more grief on his father's shoulders. But of course he loved the music Teddy Boys listened to. So, Paul being Paul, he went about things very subtly. He had his trouser bottoms taken in a little bit, and he grew his hair, but not that long. But he would never go against his father over this. In fact, it was always a point of contention between John and Paul in the early years. John would tell Paul, "Why don't you tell him to fuck off" but Paul never could.'

Yet it was Paul who was to have the biggest influence on The Beatles' public style and image. And it all began when he was twelve years old. 'The thing you have to understand about Paul,' says Mark Lewisohn, 'is that when he sees something for the first time it makes a really deep impression on him.' The McCartney family were on holiday. Paul was with his father, Jim, and his brother Mike. His mother, Mary, had been dead for about a year.

'I have a photograph of me there (Butlin's Holiday Camp) in short trousers and school blazer (You would never wear your school uniform going on holiday but I think it was all I had – my posh gear). My brother took the picture. So I was standing there in my school cap and everything, on a roasting hot day near the swimming pool, when out of the Calypso Ballroom came five guys from Gateshead. And they all looked alike. They each had on a tartan flat cap with a grey crewneck sweater, tartan shorts, pumps, and they carried white towels under their arms. They walked in a line across to the pool to have a good old swim and I noticed everyone's heads turn and go, WHO'S THAT? In that second a penny dropped for me and I realised the power of looking something. They won the talent contest at Butlin's that week for whatever they did – and you just knew that they would win.'

McCartney had just seen a five-headed monster, and his brain understood immediately the power and possibilities of uniformity. At the Woolton village fête, where Paul was famously introduced to John, John's skiffle band, The Quarrymen – named after his secondary school, Quarry Bank – were performing. But Paul so impressed John later with his guitar-playing that within a week he was a member of the band. One of the earliest shots of Paul and John performing together is highly symbolic. Looking at this photograph, the eye can't help but be drawn to Paul and John because they are wearing matching jackets. The other three are in matching shirts. McCartney had learned his lesson well. Clothes were being used to tell the world who the important ones in the band were.

ABOVE A photo taken by John Lennon of the band and others at the Arnhem War Memorial in the Netherlands: (L–R) Allan Williams (manager), his wife, Beryl, the calypso singer Lord Woodbine, Stu Sutcliffe, Paul McCartney, George Harrison and new drummer Pete Best. The inscription behind them reads: 'Their Name Liveth For Evermore.' Little did they know …

In fact, The Quarrymen often mixed up fashions. For gigs they would wear cowboy shirts with tassels coming down from the pockets and then adorn the shirt with a black bootlace tie, straight out of the Teddy Boy wardrobe. It was a trait that The Beatles would continue to exhibit throughout their career: taking the best features of every trend and then putting them satisfactorily together to create their own style.

On 29 August 1959 The Quarrymen – with McCartney, Lennon and Harrison in their ranks – opened up a new Liverpool venue called the Casbah Club. Situated in the basement of the large, rambling house of a woman named Mona Best, the club closed nearly three years later, in June 1962. By now Lennon's clothes were starting to mirror the artistic process his songwriting would be built on: that is, taking disparate styles and making them effortlessly work together.

When Mona's son Pete Best met him for the first time, Lennon was a striking mix of Teddy Boy and Beatnik – and boy, he wore it well. Just one look and Best knew instantly who the main man was.

'John looked and acted the leader from the start', he wrote in his autobiography *Beatle: The Pete Best Story*. 'He had a definitely arty look, dressed in a stark mixture of black and white; a black cord lumber jacket, a black shirt; and the whole ensemble rounded off by black and white baseball boots. All the Quarrymen wore their hair swept back from their foreheads, rocker style, but it was rather short by today's standards. The current trend was either greasy Elvis or Tony Curtis framed by the obligatory sideboards – of course, John's were longer than everyone else.'

As Pete would later discover in Amsterdam, John liked his black cord lumber jacket enormously. Not only was it stylish, but its large pockets made the coat 'ideal wear for being nimble-fingered'.

As for McCartney, Ken Brown, who would form a band with Best later that year, recalled McCartney as 'being very neat', in contrast to John's Beatnik style.

In October 1959 the band changed their name to Johnny and the Moondogs to audition for a yearly Liverpool talent show held by a man named Carroll Levis. For their look that day they wore different coloured shirts. Although they failed the audition, their use of these shirts led them seriously to consider changing their name again, this time to The Rainbows.

OPPOSITE The Silver Beetles audition for Larry Parnes and Billy Fury at the Wyvern Club. Note the band's matching shoes and clothes, save for the temporary drummer, Johnny Hutch.

Financial constraints, however, put paid to that idea. 'Though we wanted to be fashionable, the truth was that we were hard put to find enough cash to buy a proper uniform', John Lennon later recalled.

For George the day was doubly disappointing. As Billy Shepherd recalled in his book *The True Story of The Beatles*, 'the fashionable George, doyen of the dressy dressers at school, made certain that he wouldn't again be seen in the sort of corduroy jackets that the boys had managed to find for their Levis lesson in show business.' Johnny and the Moondogs went back to being The Quarrymen, and then changed the following year into The Silver Beetles.

Lennon's closest friend at the time, Stu Sutcliffe, was now the band's bass player, at John's behest. Although a highly talented painter, Sutcliffe's bass skills were sadly lacking. He would often play with his back to the audience to hide his ineptitude while other band members, such as Paul McCartney, covered for him.

By May of 1960 the group had acquired a part-time manager, named Allan Williams, who also ran the Jacaranda Club and the Wyvern (which after renovation would become the Blue Angel), two Liverpool clubs where many musicians gathered. Through his connections Williams put the group forward as a possible backing band for the singer Billy Fury.

On the day Billy Fury, his manager Larry Parnes and the band gathered at the Wyvern Club. Williams would later measure the distance between the Fury camp and The Silver Beetles in silk and after-shave. 'Larry and Billy looked like a million dollars', he recalled. 'Their after-shave lotion swamped the place and both were wearing expensive silk suits, at that time the emblem of success. I looked at The Beatles in their ragged clothes and scuffed baseball boots. They looked like something the cat dragged in on a wet night.'

Actually the band – as evidenced by a photo taken that day – did not look that bad. In keeping with the idea of a uniform, they wore dark shirts and trousers with yachting-style shoes. Only the drummer looks out of place, in his

OPPOSITE AND ABOVE The Rocker style, as modelled by this young German on his motor bike. Astrid Kirchherr and her friends Klaus Voormann and Jürgen Vollmer were fascinated by the band's Teddy Boy leanings, and Astrid soon started dating bass player Stu Sutcliffe (above left). Her photography was streets ahead of anyone else taking band photos at that time.

light-coloured shirt and casual jacket. But then the others probably didn't mind. His clothes tell us he is only temporary.

Parnes thought the band weren't suitable for Fury, but he did engage them to back another of his artists, the singer Johnny Gentle, on a short Scottish tour. Gentle got the shock of his life when they arrived.

'They arrived in jeans and sweaters and were the roughest bunch of lads I had seen in my life', he later recalled. 'John and Stu were both at art college and they looked it. Their hair fell over their collars, and Stu sported a beard. George was serving an apprenticeship and looked neat, as did Paul, who was still studying for his A levels.'

Gentle was not the only person who was struck dumb by the band's ramshackle appearance. Williams again: 'I packed them off wishing them the best of luck. In a couple of days I got an irate call from Larry Parnes. Duncan McKenna, one of the Scottish promoters, had rung him to complain about The Silver Beetles. He had told Parnes, what the heck are you doing sending me a bum group like this mob? He hadn't even heard them play! He was basing his attack on their scruffy appearance, their Marks and Sparks gear, their black sweaters and jeans and running shoes.'

In August 1960 Pete Best joined the band, on drums, and they all travelled to Hamburg for the first of their five working visits to the city. Hamburg would play a huge part in the development of the band's look, and so would clothes. In fact, within the year The Beatles would be the most radical-looking band in the UK.

Not that you would have known at the time. According to Hunter Davies, 'Their stage dress in Hamburg at this time consisted of little velvet jackets that McCartney's neighbour had made for them, worn with tight black jeans, white shirts, ribbon ties and winklepicker shoes, their hair shaped in the very fashionable Tony Curtis/Teddy Boy style.'

One night, when they were playing at a bar named the Kaiserkeller, a young German art student named Jürgen Vollmer heard the band's music from the pavement outside and decided to investigate. It took courage to do so.

Jürgen did not dress in the prevailing German style, and Hamburg could be very tough on those practising individualism. 'To tell the truth,' Jürgen would later write, 'I felt an outsider in Hamburg, which in 1960 wasn't a very tolerant place to live.' Although highly wary of the club's clientele – lots of workmen and sailors determined to have a good time, come what may – he was fascinated by The Beatles. And it wasn't only their music that was pulling him into their circle.

'We discovered later', Pete Best recalled, 'he had been drawn to these five Liverpool Teds with their Elvis-style hair and stage suits of funny little grey and white dog-tooth jackets, set off by black shirts and pants and grey winklepickers. He thought we looked somewhat ridiculous; we thought we looked the cat's whiskers.'

The next night Jürgen brought down his two friends Klaus Voormann and Astrid Kirchherr. All three were art students, and all three dressed in dark, very striking fashions.

Astrid told Radio Merseyside in 1995, 'Our philosophy then, because we were only little kids, was wearing black clothes and going around looking moody. Of course, we had a clue who Jean-Paul Sartre was. We got inspired by all the French artists and writers, because that was the closest we could get. England was so far away, and America was out of the question. So France was the nearest. So we got all the information from France, and we tried to dress like the French existentialists. … We wanted to be free, we wanted to be different, and tried to be cool, as we call it now.'

They were nicknamed the 'Exis', and as far as their clothes were concerned, anything went as long as it challenged the norm. When they laid eyes on The Beatles for the first time, straight away they recognised in their clothes the same spirit, the same thirst for the new, for the future. The look may have been different from theirs, but the fashion impulse was exactly the same: to use clothes to differentiate themselves from the rest of the world – to tell everyone, in that late '60s phrase, 'I am not a number.'

Astrid later told Hunter Davies, 'I had always been fascinated by Teddy Boys. I'd liked the look of them in photograph and films. Suddenly there were five of them in front of me, with their hair all high and long sidies. I just sat there open-mouthed and couldn't move.'

OPPOSITE Klaus Voormann looking *très chic*, *c.* 1960. Voormann would later design the sleeve for the band's *Revolver* album, using their hair as his starting-point.

The attraction was reciprocal. 'They were attracted to my looks because I looked weird then, or different', Astrid recalled. 'I used to wear black only and had very short hair. I wore these collarless jackets and leather suits, big velvet capes, boots and things like that, but I was so attracted to the way they looked with their tight jeans and leather jackets. It was a sort of give and take, from me to them, and back.'

'We all fell in love with Astrid's black leather outfits', Best confirms. 'Influenced by her, Stu (who soon began dating Astrid) was the first to appear in a black leather jacket. George soon followed suit in a jacket bought off a waiter for £5. Then the rest of us got into line, buying cheap bomber-style models which we wore with the tightest jeans and cowboy boots.

'George also discovered the cowboy boots in a shop on the Reeperbahn, creating some envy when he first turned up in a black and white pair. John and I hared off at the earliest opportunity to follow suit; Lennon chose a pair of gold and black, mine were red and black. Paul, who had a reputation amongst the group of watching his Pfennigs, stood out for some time but he eventually conformed with a black and blue pair. To top off the whole ensemble we bought pink flat caps! These seemed necessities at the time and were primarily intended to be stage outfits, although they became our everyday wear too.'

The inspiration here, says Tony Bramwell, was the singer Gene Vincent and his band the Blue Caps, whose dynamic appearance in the 1956 film *The Girl Can't Help It* made the amiable comedy drama a must-see for all rock 'n' roll fans.

It was Vincent's appearance in December 1959 on the Jack Good show *Boy Meets Girl* that cemented his image as a wild rocker. Ironically, it was Gene's gentlemanly manners at the studio that inspired Jack Good, the show's producer, to dress Gene in leather from toe to head and place a silver medallion around his neck.

Rock 'n' roll was about attitude, Good argued. No one could be that nice on TV. Gene's popularity subsequently soared. Given the paucity of music on British television at this point, one has to believe that all the music-mad Beatles were gathered round their sets as Gene went through his number. Certainly the hats the band acquired – 'twat hats' they called them – were a vigorous nod, Bramwell states, to Vincent's backing band, the Blue Caps. During their first visit to Germany, The Beatles bought leather jackets. On their second visit they wore them with leather trousers.

'Predictably, Stu was the first Beatle into leather trousers', Best reveals, telling us much about Sutcliffe's artistic and adventurous nature, a trait that The Beatles and many of their generation shared. As far as they were concerned, the world was theirs for the taking, and this confidence would be reflected in their choice of clothing.

'Astrid and he [Stu] must have been one of the earliest unisex couples on the fashion scene', according to Best. 'They even had matching pale complexions. It wasn't all that long – as soon as we could afford it, in fact – before the rest of the Beatles were draping their legs in black leather and looking for longer jackets to replace the bomber-style models now showing signs of wear. Our gear, however, was strictly downmarket compared with Astrid and Stu's.'

That's because, according to Tony Bramwell, 'The leather jackets and trousers came from C & A in Hamburg and Liverpool.' (C & A is a downmarket clothing store.)

Again, Pete Best: 'I was the first to buy a longer leather coat in a shop at the end of the Grosse Freiheit. When Lennon saw it, he could hardly wait to follow suit. "Great," he exclaimed, "Where did you get it? How much?" It had cost about £15. The next day he collected his Marks together and got into line. George joined in the new look as well, but Paul had yet to make a move. ... There was only one thing to do.

'We all paraded in front of him and told him it was now up to him to buy a longer coat. "This is our new image" it was impressed on him, but he still wasn't keen. In the end we had to escort him to the shop. "This guy wants a cloak like ours", the assistant was told. "Size 38–40."'

OPPOSITE George taking a break from guitar duties at the Cavern Club, Liverpool, *c.* 1960.

FOLLOWING PAGES · LEFT Lennon, McCartney and Best at the Cavern Club in 1962, still wearing leather clothes. The heat generated by their Cavern shows would be one of the compelling reasons for the band to move into cooler mohair clothing. Better wages was another.

RIGHT John Lennon in typical combative action. After honing their skills during their residency in Hamburg, they became the best live band in Liverpool.

the
BEATLES

LEFT John Lennon looking wistful and moody in leather for Astrid's camera.

OPPOSITE · ABOVE The band perform in matching leather jackets in Liverpool in 1962, just prior to signing their EMI recording contract.

BELOW Thanks to manager Brian Epstein's insistence, the leather clothes have gone now, and the band return to Hamburg in suits in December 1962.

Although leather jackets and trousers in the UK were associated with the rockers – primarily, working-class men who adored motor cycles, wore heavy leather jackets, loved Jerry Lee Lewis and brassy blondes and saw themselves as firm outsiders – leather also had sexual connotations.

Given that The Beatles were by now sleeping with numerous women, their leather clothes were a reflection of the sexual freedom they were enjoying in clubs such as the Indra and the Star. Although none of them was a virgin by the time they reached Hamburg, Liverpool had no equivalent to Hamburg's licentious red-light district. In Hamburg, The Beatles were liberated from all constrictions. In Hamburg they were handed the Holy Trinity of sex and drugs and rock 'n' roll, and they worshipped at those altars on a very regular basis.

The leather look, then – the rebel look, if you like – not only marked them out but also served to give them a real sense of liberation, which they revelled in. Not everyone was knocked out by their style, though. They once trooped off to musician Bert Kaempfert's house to discuss a collaboration. Bert was out, and his door was opened by his housemaid. Taking one look at their collective image, she steadfastly refused to let them into the house until Bert arrived.

'I wouldn't let them into the living room', she later recalled. 'I stood them on the patio and gave them some drinks.'

Others were far more welcoming, especially the regulars at their shows.

'They liked us because we were kind of rough', George Harrison recalled. 'There were all these other acts going dum de dum de dum and suddenly we would come on jumping and stomping in these wild leathers suits. ... So that became our band uniform: cowboy boots, twat hats and black leather suits.'

Where the cowboy boots were concerned, there is a pragmatic element to consider. As Beatle expert Mark Lewisohn explains, 'The cowboy boots were essential to their act. If you went to see The Beatles at the start of 1961, what you saw was a group that stomped a lot. They were like Slade ten years before their time. The cowboy boots were part of that. They have got wooden heels and they are on wooden stages.'

When The Beatles returned to Liverpool, not only were they a finely honed band, capable of playing energetic four-hour sets with a real intensity, but they were also the most radical-looking band in the country, completely at odds with the prevailing rules that governed the entertainment world.

The commandments had been set in stone and observed for many years. Anyone walking out on stage would do so in a smart suit with a tie. They would have short hair and they would be clean-shaven. They would be everything – in other words – that The Beatles were not at this point in their career.

That they stood for the new and not the old Britain can be gleaned from an encounter that John had with his Aunt Mimi over a – symbolic, I would venture – piece of clothing. Having returned from Hamburg with some money in his pocket, Lennon took his girlfriend Cynthia out on a shopping spree. 'He'd seen all kinds of fantastic leather clothes in Germany and he wanted me to have a leather coat', she writes in her autobiography. 'We headed for C & A Modes, a large department store in the centre of town, where we scoured their long racks of coats. Black was John's first choice of colour for me, but as there wasn't one in my size, we chose a gorgeous three-quarter-length chocolate brown one for £17. It was my first present from him and I felt so gorgeous in it I couldn't wait to show it off. We went to visit Mimi. There was a delicatessen called Cooper's next door to C & A, so we bought her a cooked chicken for tea and set off, full of high spirits. ... When she saw that coat and heard that John had bought it for me, she hit the roof. She screamed at John that he had spent his money on a gangster's moll and hurled first the chicken, which she grabbed from me, then a hand mirror at John.'

For John, for the new generation, life meant living for the moment, not saving for a future that might not happen, an attitude that was totally at odds with the careful, risk-free approach to life that a lot of Aunt Mimi's generation tended to take.

The Beatles were out to change this approach, with its rules and regulations. They stood for progress, not conformity, and they knew they had to stick to their guns. As Lennon would later tell the magazine *Fab 208*, 'Our whole success has been due to the fact that we are "different" – a complete change from what people generally imagine pop stars to be. I don't want to an all-round entertainer. I want to be somebody people recognise as having real talent.'

Cilla Black played with the band in the St John's Hall in Liverpool in 1960. She later recalled that night to *Fab 208* and did so with a real shudder. 'Honestly, I had the shock of my life. They had these pink leather coats and those funny caps. The sound was FAB but the clothes were worse than ever. I mean I knew they were clever boys ... but I thought only madmen would wear clothes like that ... I couldn't help thinking again something was wrong when such sensible people could dress so atrociously.'

Bob Wooler, the DJ at the Cavern, where The Beatles had now started playing the first of their 274 shows at the venue, recalls: 'First impressions? Well, they were dishevelled and unkempt. They looked sort of Beatnik-y with leather jackets and faded jeans. People thought they were German. Their hair was long then, but not in the style they have it now. It just went anywhere more or less. Their attitude was that they liked what they were doing and you could take it or leave it.'

The young Cavern club audience had no qualms. They thrilled to the band's insouciance and arrogance, a haughty attitude filtered through their clothes. Liz Hughes was a Cavern regular. She recalls: 'They were always in their leather jackets, jeans, Cuban heels and their hair everywhere. It was so different from the run-of-the-mill groups at the time with their suede-collared jackets and matching colours, all blues and yellows. These four lads just came on in anything. Whatever they happened to get up in that morning they played in that day. And I think the kids just took to them because they were working-class.'

On 6 July 1961 Bill Harry, Lennon's old college friend, began the *Mersey Beat* newspaper, dedicated to covering the burgeoning Liverpool scene. In the first edition John donated a typically witty and surreal article entitled, 'Being A Short Diversion On The Dubious Origins Of Beatles, Translated From The [*sic*] John Lennon'.

Art one point he writes, 'So suddenly all back in Liverpool Village', Lennon wrote, 'were many groups playing in grey suits and Jim [McCartney, Paul's dad] said, "Why have you no grey suits" "We don't like them, Jim", we said.'

It is telling that he takes time out to defend the band's style. Certainly, the band's parents and guardians – strict but loving people – would not have been taken with the idea of seeing their charges dressed in threatening black leather.

But if the leather look was accepted by their audience, it also served a very important purpose: it instantly separated the band from every other group playing in Liverpool at that time. As the number of such groups exceeded four hundred, it was an important move to make. The leathers put The Beatles in a place of their own, one they guarded jealously and never vacated.

Later on in life, when success was raining down on them, Paul McCartney told the writer Billy Shepherd, 'Now we don't want to sound a bit big-time, but what happened was that a lot of the other groups decided to wear the same sort of stuff, so we were back with the common herd, as it were. That didn't suit us at all.' The key words there are 'common herd' and 'that didn't suit us at all'.

In October an aunt gave Lennon the huge sum of £100 for his twenty-first birthday. He told Paul he was treating him to a holiday in Spain. They had experienced Germany; now it was time to investigate further.

The excited boys decided to hitch-hike, to be like Kerouac on the road, but more importantly to save money. McCartney now put forward an idea – he and John would wear bowler hats while hitching. It was a smart idea.

In 1961 the bowler hat was the ultimate symbol of mainstream success. Working-class men wore flat caps, but Prime Ministers and prominent businessmen wore bowlers to big offices in big cities. McCartney saw that two young ruffians in leather jackets and jeans wearing bowlers would create such a spectacle on the roads that intrigued drivers would pull over out of sheer curiosity. And he wasn't wrong.

'We still had our leather jackets and drainpipes – we were too proud of them not to wear them in case we met a girl', Macca later recalled. 'And if we did meet a girl, then off came the bowlers. But for the lifts we put the bowlers on. Two guys in bowler hats – a lorry would stop! Sense of humour. This and the train is how we got to Paris.'

On arrival in the French capital, the boys spent a night in a cheap hotel. The next day they decided they could not face the last leg of their journey. They also knew that their old friend Jürgen Vollmer was in town, and by accessing him they could access Paris. This change of plan would prove to be a fortuitous twist

ABOVE An early shot of Ringo's previous band, Rory Storm and the Hurricanes, with Ringo standing far right. Note how Rory wears a different-coloured suit in order to stand out from the rest of the band, a trick used by many singers at the time.

OPPOSITE · LEFT Ringo as a Teddy Boy, a fashion he had to adopt to avoid being beaten up every time he stepped outside the house.

RIGHT George, John and Paul posing at Paul's house, 20 Forthlin Road, Liverpool, where hundreds of songs were written before the band took over the world.

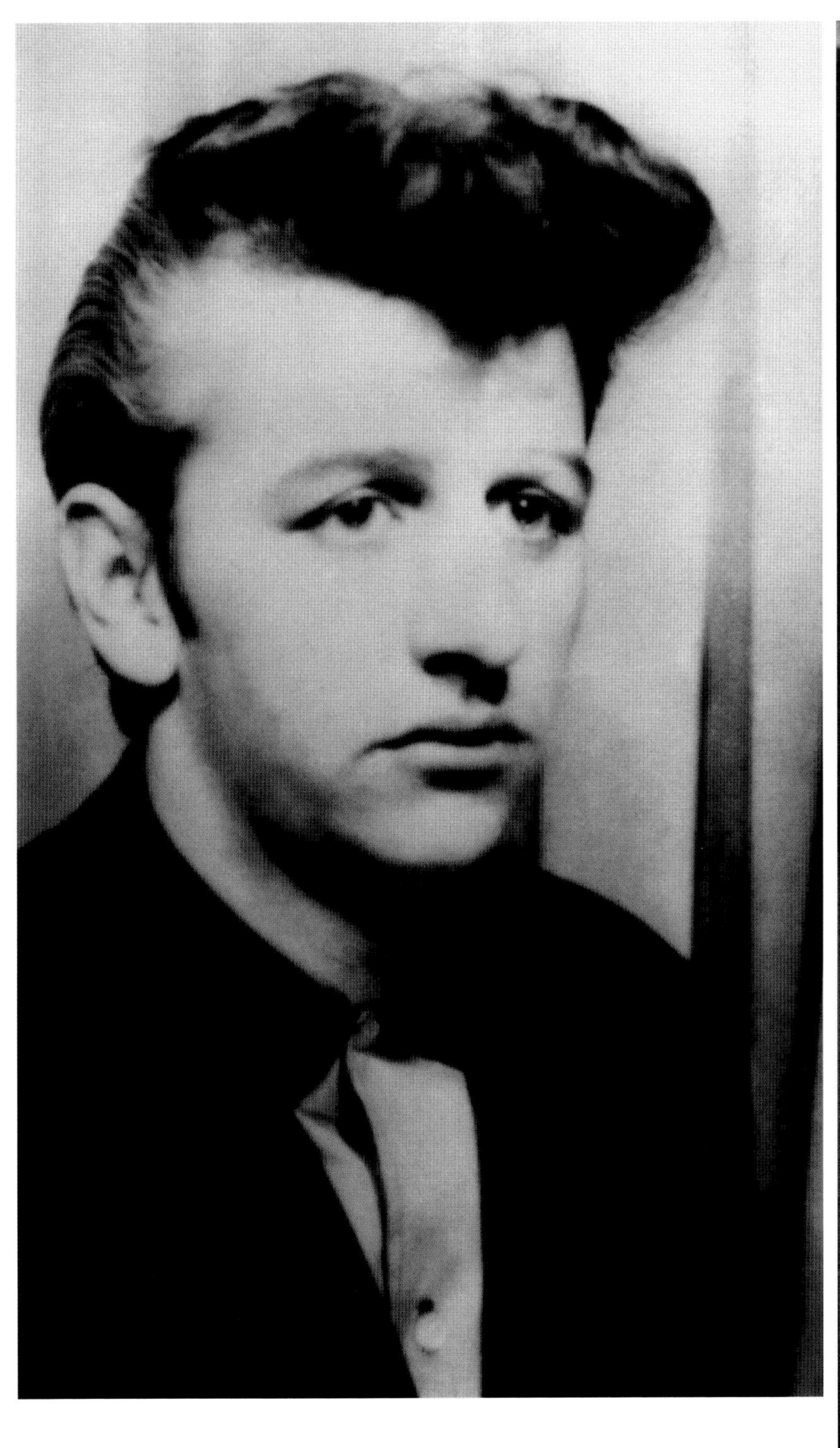

of fate. Fashion-wise, the effect would prove spectacular. John Lennon and Paul McCartney were about to have their heads turned 360 degrees.

McCartney: 'We saw guys walking round in short leather jackets and very wide pantaloons. Talk about fashion! This was going to kill them when we got back. This was totally happening. They were tight to the knee and then they flared out, they must have been fifty inches around the bottom and our drainpipe trousers must have been something like fifteen or sixteen. (Fifteen were the best, but you couldn't really get your feet through at fifteen so sixteen was acceptable.)'

John and Paul bought a pair each and spent the day wandering round Paris with Jürgen, trying out their new trousers. Much as they wanted to fit in, they just did not feel comfortable. After years of wearing their favoured 'drainies' this was a flare too far. Plus, they knew that back home in Liverpool, pantaloons would incite a riot and violent accusations of homosexuality.

'We didn't want to appear feminine or anything like that,' John recalled, 'because our audience in Liverpool still had a lot of fellas.'

The boys reverted to their leather jackets and jeans, and Jürgen suggested they meet his very good-looking girlfriend at a café one afternoon. When the girlfriend arrived, she took one look at Paul and John and then launched into a fierce tirade aimed at Jürgen. What was he thinking? How dare he even dream of introducing her to such horrible slobs?

Jürgen hit back, called her a narrow-minded bourgeois, and she stormed off, never to be seen again. But the lesson was quickly learned. If John and Paul were going to succeed with the Mademoiselles, they were going to have to change their image. Jürgen accordingly took them to a flea market, where they bought jackets – green corduroy for John, dark-coloured artist-style jacket for Paul. This was not to be the last time they changed clothes to gain a bigger prize. In two months time a man called Brian Epstein would ask them to act in exactly the same way.

OPPOSITE The very dapper Mr Brian Epstein. It was Epstein's wealth and acumen, as expressed through his immaculate style, that quickly convinced The Beatles to take him on as their manager.

Meanwhile, Jürgen went in completely the opposite direction. He bought himself a leather jacket. 'At that time nobody but rockers wore the symbol of the working-class rebel,' he wrote, 'and I felt as revolutionary as John and Paul must have felt in their new artsy outfits.'

According to Neil Aspinall, the band's road manager, writing in *Fab 208* a few years later, during this trip John and Paul spent most of their money on clothing. Paul even bought himself a plastic police cape, which he treasured for years.

On their way home the two boys stopped off in London. In Covent Garden they come across a shop named Anello & Davide. Opened in 1922, the shop's business is to supply bespoke dance shoes to theatres. Of late, however, their designs had become fashionable streetwear.

John and Paul were entranced by the shop's window display, especially a Chelsea-style boot placed towards the back. The first rule of smart dressing is you always begin with the shoes. John and Paul went in and ordered a couple of pairs, but with a proviso – they wanted a Cuban heel added to the design.

Pete Best remembers John arriving back in Liverpool and declaring of these shoes, '"I fell in love with them and just had to get some. So did Paul" – and so did we all after they swaggered back to Merseyside.'

Holiday over, the Beatles resumed their live engagements and did so with great confidence. 'We were, to put it mildly, different', McCartney recalled. 'We looked like a gang of scruffs. We were probably the most untidy group in the business. It was the leather bit with us. We had all these ill-matching outfits with jeans setting off the scruffiness of our coats and boots. Nothing tidy for us. We figured that if the German teenagers had gone for the stamp and shout stuff, then we stood a chance in Liverpool.'

On 9 November 1961 the manager of the NEMS record store, Brian Epstein, took his assistant, Alastair Taylor, to see The Beatles play a lunchtime show at the Cavern. Afterwards he went to see the band backstage. After a swift hello, he departed. George Harrison watched him leave and then turned to his band mates and said in admiring tones, 'Did you see his suit?'

'And his shiny shoes', someone else chimed in.

USUAL PRICE
SALE PRICE
USUAL PRICE 69/11
SALE PRICE
45/-
USUAL PRICE 89/6
SALE PRICE
49/-
SIZE 11
USUAL PRICE 49/11
SALE PRICE
REAL SUEDE
20/-
6. 6½ 7 8
USUAL PRICE
SALE PRICE
35/11
USUAL PRICE
SALE PRICE
35/11
ALL SIZES
USUAL PRICE 99/6
SALE PRICE
ANALINE CALF
49/-
SIZE 6½
USUAL PRICE 63/-
SALE PRICE
39/-
10½ 11
USUAL PRICE 49/11
SALE PRICE
39/-
USUAL PRICE 99/6
SALE PRICE
35/-
7. 7½. 8. 9
USUAL PRICE 105/-
SALE PRICE
39/-
SIZE 6½
USUAL PRICE 119/6
SALE PRICE
FLEXIBLE
59/-
SIZE 8. 8½
USUAL PRICE 119/-
SALE PRICE
55/-
6½ 7 8

IT'S ONLY BEATLEMANIA
Chapter Two

That's it, I'm not a Beatle any more.

GEORGE HARRISON

In the Liverpool of the young Beatles the tailoring business boomed. Everyone wore suits and jackets and trousers, and someone had to make them, care for them, tend to them. Demand exceeded supply. On any given Saturday, Burton's and several other large menswear outfitters would take on six extra staff just to deal with the queues forming outside their shops.

Jeans had yet to make an impact on the fashion landscape. If they were worn, it was always by the young, and they had the actors Marlon Brando and James Dean in mind – especially Dean – when they pulled them on.

Dean was the youthful malcontent from the 1955 film *Rebel without a Cause*, the conflicted jean-wearing cat whose sneer and Brylcreem anguish captivated many young souls.

'A lot of the kids bought jeans with the trouser leg a little too long so your mum could make a turn-up out of it and then you could look like James Dean', Billy Hatton recalls. 'Back then cinema gave the young their view of the world. We all copied that stuff until The Beatles made it over there. And then they started copying us.' He raises his fist in triumph. 'We got our own back then.' (To illustrate the contempt the adult world felt for jeans, which were seen as work clothing, Paul McCartney was one day denied entry to the Cavern – hardly the swankiest joint in town. Part of the problem was that jeans were American, and many felt aggravated by America swiping all the glory for the defeat of Hitler in the Second World War.)

If you had the money, great, a top-quality handmade suit was all yours. Otherwise you had two choices. One was to go 'on the drip' – Liverpool slang for hire purchase. 'You would go to the tailor,' Billy Hatton reveals, 'get a little book and you would go in every week and pay him whatever you had agreed to pay and you would pay for your clothes that way. At least that allowed the youngsters to dress their way, which made a big difference.'

If 'the drip' was not an option, then you then dropped a level and bought a cheap off-the-peg number, which you slipped into any one of the numerous alteration shops dotted around town and had changed into your vision.

OPPOSITE In 1961 John and Paul bought boots from the famous Anello & Davide shop in London. By 1963 the 'Beatle boot' was one of the most famous items of footwear in Britain.

'There were loads of outworkers', the tailor Walter Smith confirms. 'You'd have waistcoat-makers, coat-makers. Round this city there'd be about twenty little tailoring workshops, there'd be lads after school running round the city with a bag or cover, with an armful of trousers of waistcoats, taking things backwards and forwards. It was amazing, the opportunities for young fellas in those days.'

Clothes did not come cheap, though. In April 1961 a suit put you back 10 guineas (£10 and 10 shillings), a suit jacket £7 and a shirt – say, a poplin number – 39 shillings and 6 pence. And eye-catching items such as Scottish knitwear? That will be 40 shillings, please sir. A handmade suit would take a minimum of £28 from your wage packet, at a time when the national wage was around £15 a week.

No wonder the two tailors who dominated Liverpool, Hyman Jacobs and Beno Dorn, were both located in the Wirral, one of Merseyside's most affluent areas. Walter Smith, The Beatles' first tailor, worked for both firms. He started at Jacobs in 1949 before moving over to Beno Dorn in 1951. He was chastised for doing so; the two firms were fierce rivals, always looking to outdo one another.

One of Walter's regular clients was a man he warmed to, a man named Brian Epstein. Born on 19 September 1934 into a prosperous family, Epstein was well known for his elegant style of dress. Not surprisingly, his look exuded wealth and class.

'He wore sheer black nylon socks', Shelagh Johnston, an ex-employee recalls. 'I remember thinking – gosh, such wealth and prosperity.'

His biographer Ray Coleman wrote that Brian was 'Perhaps Liverpool's best-dressed bachelor. His thick hair was styled at the Horne Brothers salon, and his clothes came from the top tailors.' One of those top tailors, George Hayes, would later (in great admiration) remark, 'He always looked like he had just stepped out of the bath.'

Although his family owned and ran the NEMS record store on Liverpool's Whitechapel Road, Epstein, at fifteen, developed other dreams; he announced that a dress designer he would be. He was swiftly relieved of this wild ambition.

'Father did not want me to be a dress designer because he thought it was a rather dodgy business and we had a stable family business waiting', he told Derek Taylor for his biography, *A Cellar Full of Noise*. 'Also he thought it wasn't manly. Also I thought myself it might not be good because I loathe being second-best at anything. I wanted to be Christian Dior.'

As Epstein's career unravelled – army, family business – his love of clothes and his ability to look smart and pristine at all times never wavered. He wore Burberry raincoats long before they were popular. He shopped at high-class stores such as Watson and Prickard, buying polka-dot cravats as well as blazers and a bowler hat. Such was his style, it is hard to imagine Epstein as a carefree teenager. His clothes aged him. It was a very grown-up British style.

'He had definite ideas about style, trouser widths and lapels', says Dennis Goodman, who often served Brian at Watson and Prickard.

Those definite ideas he would now hand to The Beatles. Ironically, Epstein and the band had already crossed paths – thanks to clothes. Brian first noticed the band in his record shop. They had probably just played a lunchtime Cavern show. 'Every afternoon,' he said, according to Coleman's biography, 'a group of scruffy leather-jacketed lads came in. Strange and odd, but attractive. I thought at one time they were messing around with the girls and I asked the girls. The girls said they did buy discs and they knew what they wanted. They bought r'n'b.'

Subconsciously, there had also been contact. In 1961 The Beatles had been featured on the cover of *Mersey Beat*, a paper sold every week in Epstein's shop.

Clothes played a crucial part in Brian's initial relationship with the band. His immaculate look, the sophisticated way he carried himself, quickly convinced The Beatles that he was the right manager for them.

'To us, Brian was the expert', John Lennon said.

George Harrison concurred. 'Brian Epstein was from an upper-middle-class background and he wanted us to appeal to the producers of radio, television and record companies.'

On 3 December 1961 Epstein became the band's manager. One of the first things he told them was that, if they were serious about making it, then the leathers and the louche on-stage antics would have to go. No point going forward otherwise. He loved the band, but their stage behaviour beggared belief. Often they would smoke and drink and even eat on stage while chatting informally to the audience, and it was wrong and had to stop.

'We used to have marvellous raves down at the Cavern', Paul McCartney recalls. 'We had to keep ourselves laughing. We used to come on with the maddest gear on. I had shredded newspaper sticking out of the bottom of my trouser legs, John wore a cellophane bag around his shoes and we came on wearing collars and ties and nothing else above the waist.'

No longer. On stage the band would act with decorum and wear proper suits. In Beatle history this move into suits is a contentious area. Some believe that the suits symbolise the decline of the band's purity, that this is where the band were neutered. Lennon certainly said as much in many interviews. 'He literally fucking cleaned us up!' he shouted at one interviewer.

Yet Lennon should never be taken at face value. He was far too capricious. Mark Lewisohn explains: 'It always depends on who he is talking to and what mood he is in. One minute he will think he sold out and the next he will understand why it happened. One day he jumps only to the bottom line and on other days he will look at the steps of how he got there and realise that is the way he was going.'

Thus, one minute Lennon would be pro-suit, and the next he would be highly dismissive. 'Outside of Liverpool, when we went down South in our leather outfits,' he once explained, 'the dance hall promoters really didn't like us. They thought we looked like a gang of thugs. So it got to be Epstein saying, "Look if you wear a suit you will get this much money" and everybody wanted a good sharp black suit. We liked the leather and the jeans but we wanted a good suit even to wear off stage. "Yeah man, all right, I'll wear a suit – I'll wear a bloody balloon if somebody is going to pay me." I'm not in love with leather that much.' But on another occasion he remarked: 'I saw a film of the first television we ever did. The Granada people came down to film us and there we were in the suits and it just wasn't us. Watching that film, I knew that was where we started to sell out.'

OPPOSITE AND FOLLOWING PAGE The band in matching mohair suits and serious expressions, posing for Astrid Kirchherr's camera in Hamburg

Two men who would be associated with The Beatles for a long time, Derek Taylor and Pete Shotton, vigorously challenge John's anti-suit stance. Shotton said: 'Despite John's complaint (voiced a decade or so later) that Brian had forced the Beatles to "sell out", Brian was obviously incapable of making John do anything John didn't wish to do. In 1962 and 1963 the number one priority on John's agenda was to become rich and famous, and tidying up his image seemed, at the time, a relatively small price to pay for the attainment of that goal.'

Derek Taylor: 'There was a lot of posthumous wise-after-the-event stuff like John saying he [Epstein] shouldn't have put them in suits, that it was a big sell-out etc. They didn't mind at the time. They were making more money that way and they were starting to think that the leather thing was out anyway.'

Certainly neither McCartney nor Harrison nor Pete Best ever expressed any anti-suit sentiments. In fact they welcomed Epstein's idea, and there were plenty of reasons for doing so.

To begin with, playing long, energetic rock 'n' roll sets in leather clothing in a steaming hot place like the Cavern was not the most practical idea. Also, by 1961 rockers were becoming passé and the band's restless creativity would have demanded something new to satisfy itself with. Moreover, it was time to look much further afield. Liverpool belonged to The Beatles, but only Liverpool. It was time to claim the rest of the world, and if mohair suits facilitated that achievement, then so much the better.

'I didn't think it was a bad idea,' McCartney recalled, 'because it fitted with my Gateshead group philosophy that you should look similar, and because we got mohair suits it was a bit like the black acts. It was later put about that I had betrayed our leather image but, as I recall, I didn't actually have to drag anyone to the tailors. We all went quite happily over the water to the Wirral to Beno Dorn, a little tailor who made mohair suits. That started to change the image a little and though we would still wear leather occasionally, for the posh do's we would put on the suits.'

Interesting that Macca should mention black acts, as the band's musical attention at this juncture was increasingly being taken by the developing new r'n'b records issued by Tamla Motown, Atlantic and other labels.

A lot of this music was delivered by men draped in elegant suits and ties. One of John's favourite bands, The Miracles, were the epitome of this style. In fact, John's song 'This Boy' was directly influenced by the Miracles and was delivered by Lennon in a sharp suit and his best haircut to millions of Americans on 16 February 1964 on the *Ed Sullivan Show*.

After Epstein had told Walter Smith, his tailor, that he was bringing in The Beatles, Smith went upstairs and asked if anyone present had heard of the band. Yes, they play at the Cavern, he was told.

'And my comment was "They'll never get anywhere with a name like that"', Smith says self-deprecatingly. He is sitting in the front space of his shop, Craft Tailoring, in Liverpool, still tailoring, still guiding people in matters of style.

'I fixed them up with the cloth,' Smith recalls, 'and there was some haggling over the price. It was 28 guineas. Brian Epstein said, "It's too expensive", so I said to Mr Dorn, "Mr Epstein likes this for this group but he thinks it's too expensive", and he said, "Give them 3 guineas discount", so it was 25 guineas. Brian was paying, and I remember they had strong ideas of what they wanted.

'First they wanted the drop shoulder, slightly boxy short jackets and trousers absolutely narrow. If you look at that picture it will tell you, it's almost the size of their ankles – fourteen I think. We narrowed the trousers. In fact, they twice sent the trousers back, asking them to be tightened even more. I couldn't believe how narrow they wanted them.'

Epstein was not interested in the band copying others. He encouraged his boys to do what they would do throughout their career – subvert the norm. This they did by insisting their trousers adopt the drainpipe style that they had so adored as teenagers. It was a subtle move and, given the attention the band paid to the making and shaping of their suits, one does not detect a group being forced to act against its will. For some Beatle fans the mohair suits signalled the start of the band's eventual departure from Liverpool, and that caused resentment. For others, such as Cavern DJ Bob Wooler, the mohair suits were impractical.

'I was at the Cavern, and I announced to the audience, "The Beatles will be appearing soon in their new suits for the very first time on Merseyside tonight"', he later remembered. 'Of course, it was jam-packed. It was a sweatbox and everyone sweated. They went on stage and really sweated and all their suits began to rot, they began to come apart at the seams. The Beatles said to Brian this is ridiculous. He was furious because he had not got sweat-proof suits. But that was the start of the new image. They learned how to adjust.'

It took some time, though. At another gig, according to Pete Best, John viciously tore into Epstein.

'Our first stage suits were shiny dark blue mohair which had been purchased for our first night club date in Liverpool's Cabaret Club, an engagement arranged by Epstein. This was an upmarket venue and not the kind of place we had been used to. Lennon was in rebellious mood, already having voiced the opinion that our new manager was trying to turn us into Little Lord Fauntleroys.

'When John saw the club's multicoloured check flooring he could contain himself no longer ... "With all the lights and reflection we will look like bloody rainbows. You just manage us, don't try to re-design us. People want to see The Beatles. This isn't The Beatles." Which was true. We were at home in our leathers, we liked to be casual. Suits and collars and ties were for people who worked in offices.'

Tony Bramwell states that the band's shirts were made by a Swedish company called Melka and were chosen because of their durability and versatility. Every night they could be washed in a basin, hung up and ready the very next morning.

Bramwell also recalls that in Liverpool 'In those days there was a Lord's Day Observance Society that ran a strict ruling on ballrooms, clubs and theatres. You couldn't wear make-up or costumes on a Sunday, so on a lot of occasions we had to be seen walking down the street in the suits so as to show this is what we were wearing. Inside the theatre we then used make-up.'

In June 1962 the band signed to EMI and began a famous and long-lasting relationship with the producer George Martin. On first meeting him, the band thought Martin posh, like a schoolteacher. He in turn thought them raw, although not without promise. It was the subject of clothes that broke the ice.

George Harrison recalls: 'He was explaining things and he said, "Is there anything you are not happy about?" We shuffled about silently and then I said, 'Well ... I don't like your tie." There was a moment of "Ohhhhh" but then he laughed and we did too.'

In 1963 Beatlemania was born, and among other things it was that kind of cheek – humorous but never nasty – that the country would find such a tonic. What Liverpool had adored for years now became national property. The band's music and look captivated the nation. A telling symbol of this phenomenon is the brief change that took place in Epstein's own clothing.

Not long into his association with the band Epstein suddenly dropped his suave, sophisticated look and started appearing at gigs dressed like a Beatle, in a poloneck sweater, dark jeans and leather jacket.

When he first did it, says Pete Best, Lennon's acid tongue went into overdrive. 'Look! He changes us into suits and now he wants to be one of us.' Lennon raged at one gig.

'Eppy blushed red, clenched his fists and was silent for some seconds', the ex-Beatle drummer writes. 'Then very politely he said, "Well, it's casual isn't it?"'

In Ray Coleman's book a similar incident is described. Epstein arrived for a show at the Orrell Park Ballroom in Bootle, just north of Liverpool, and such was his casual style that 'The doorman refused to believe he was the manager of The Beatles and would not let him in. He quickly reverted to suits and ties', Coleman writes.

Despite the highly differing backgrounds of manager and band, the Beatles' music and character were so intoxicating, so compelling, they had the power to smash through all class barriers. For 'Epstein', read 'Britain'. Even the Queen would soon be exposed to Beatleworld.

As national fame spread around them, the band's image was constantly remarked on by the press. No one had seen a band like The Beatles before. The Beatles were four characters who had come together to make one amazing whole. Clothes, therefore, were incredibly important in establishing this groundbreaking principle. Not only did clothes unite them, but they also created a complete entity: the

OPPOSITE The style of Motown acts such as The Miracles exerted a strong influence on the band, as these photos testify.

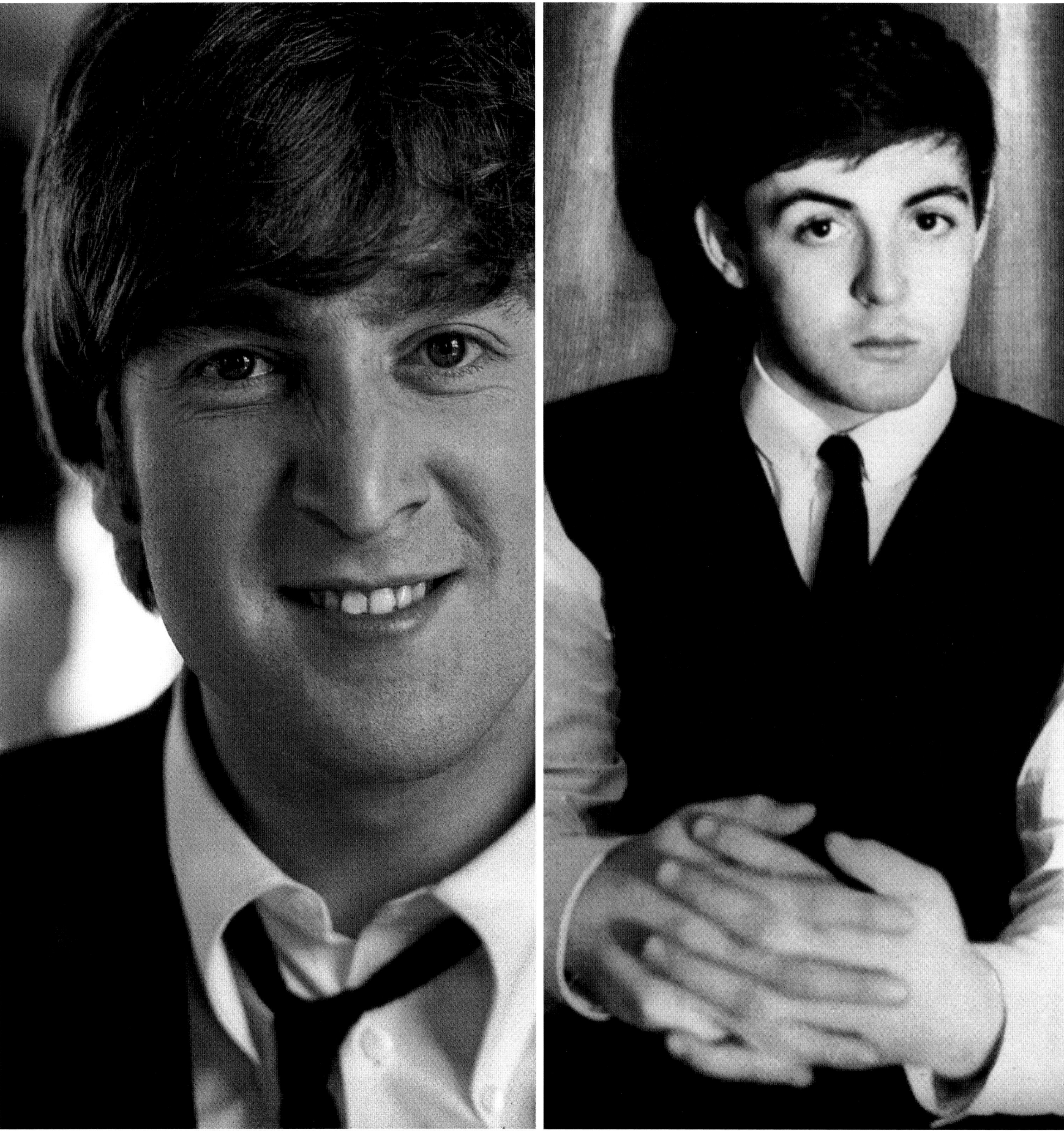

OPPOSITE · LEFT John with his tie a little askew, a subversion that many believe symbolised his dislike of the band's move away from leathers and into suits. This was strongly denied by the band themselves.

RIGHT Throughout his whole Beatle career Paul would do much to popularise the tank top.

ABOVE An early shot of the band that would conquer the world.

ABOVE In contrast to their friends and main rivals, the Rolling Stones, The Beatles' smiling image, good looks and smart clothes did much to attract hordes of young girls to their cause, giving rise to the phenomenon known as Beatlemania.

four-headed monster, no less. Recall again Lennon's quote about success being achieved 'because we are different'.

The fact that they dressed for themselves – and therefore for their fans – created a unique sense of togetherness between the band and their audience which had never been witnessed before. The obvious care the band now took in their presentation was a quality every woman could relate to. Read the – mainly female – fans' testimonies from that time. They often used the phrase 'They were one of us.' It is why Liverpool grieved and resented The Beatles' worldwide success. When national success hit, their bestest friends in the whole wide world moved abroad, for ever, and the Liverpool lass was left sobbing into her pillow.

Maureen Cleave (*Evening Standard*, 2 February 1963): 'I think it's their looks that really get people going, that starts the girls queuing up outside the Liverpool Grafton at 5.30 for 8 p.m. Their average age is twenty and they have what their manager likes to call "exceptional taste in clothes". They look scruffy but scruffy on purpose.

'They wear bell-bottom suits of a rich burgundy colour with black velvet collars. Boots, of course. Shoes seem to have died out all together.'

It is notable that Cleave should call them scruffy. From our vantage point they look anything but scruffy, but to Cleave's eye, conditioned by her era and the high prevalence of suits, the Beatle uniforms in no way measured up to the standard set by the rich or royalty. But then what price Cleave's instincts, when she confuses bell-bottom trousers with the drainpipe style?

Derek Taylor's review of the band in the *Manchester Evening News* on 30 May 1963 stated: "When the no-lapelled, shiny black suits and thick black Roman haircuts of the stars appeared to a cascade of outrageous praise from the compère, the cinema went wild. Nobody could hear themselves trying to think. The act was largely wooden but it didn't matter at all.' Taylor would later write that the all-round entertainer Frankie Vaughan was 'everything The Beatles were not – restrained, formally polite, respectful, conformist, monogamous and professional.'

With national fame came all kinds of offers. One of them was from a Liverpool jeans company called Libro, which approached Epstein; for a large amount of money the band agreed to advertise their jeans.

'Libro made four different jeans for the band', Tony Bramwell recalls. 'Paul's were dog-tooth, John's striped, Ringo's were black and George's royal blue. The band hated the jeans. They were hideous.'

The huge importance the band placed on always looking Fab can be gauged from the fact that the Libro affair was the first and last time The Beatles would ever advertise anyone else's products.

In the summer of 1963 the band bade Liverpool farewell and moved to London. Brian Epstein now chose them a new tailor. His name was Dougie Millings, and it made perfect sense – Millings was the 'tailor to the stars'.

Born in Manchester on 30 July 1913, Millings learned the complexities of bespoke tailoring at Leith Academy in Edinburgh before undertaking a tailoring apprenticeship at a department store there. He then moved to Leeds, before arriving in London in the 1930s. By day he worked as a tailor's cutter at Hector Powe in Regent Street. By night he boosted his earnings by performing as a crooner. That is why a guitar is hung on the wall of his tailoring shop at 63 Old Compton Street. Often he would bring the guitar down and have his pop star client hold the guitar as he measured him. That way, when the musician was performing, his suit would be sure not to roll up at the arms. It was such touches, coupled with his great talents, that got him noticed.

His first pop star customer was Cliff Richard, who had made his name at the famous Two I's coffee bar, just up the road from Millings. After Cliff, Millings went on to make several famous items, including many for visiting American musicians. These included making plaid jackets for Bill Haley and the Comets, Roy Orbison's black suits with concealed zip fastening, and Wee Willie Harris's red-and-pink suit. He also put together Billy Fury's gold lamé suit.

Millings's first suits for The Beatles are nicely described by Ray Coleman. 'From twelve ounce mohair and worsted material,' Coleman writes, 'Millings created a style envied by other stars for its simplicity and uniqueness and which Epstein

ABOVE AND RIGHT London Mods, whose emphasis on sharp clothing and love of American r'n'b chimed strongly with The Beatles' own tastes in fashion and music.

applauded: a four-button, high-buttoning jacket in dark grey, with black velvet collar and no outside pleats. There were eight-inch side-pleats in the jacket, cut with a tubular look, the shoulders as narrow as each Beatle could carry. The skin-tight trousers were so tight the Beatles could hardly sit down in them. Brian ordered that several suits of the same colours should be made to cope with emergencies and chose the same colours. The suits were made in silver grey, blue, navy blue, beige and black.'

By now The Beatles were the most written- and talked-about band in the country, and their clothes magnificently reflected their exalted status. Not long after settling in the capital they bumped into Rolling Stones' manager, Andrew Loog Oldham. The band would see the Stones at the Station Hotel, Richmond, all four of them entering the club dressed identically in long leather coats. They stood at the back, imperious and of the moment.

Oldham is a true stylist. He tends to remember events by the clothes he or those present were wearing. In his autobiography, *Stoned*, he recalls: 'John and Paul were fabulous in their three-piece, four-button, bespoke Dougie Millings suits. With Paul in lighter and John in darker shades of grey, their gear was a Mod variation of the Ted drape jacket, with black velvet collars, slash pockets and narrow, plain-front trousers.'

(The early Stones tried to copy the Beatles, posing in dog-tooth jackets with velvet collars for the magazine *Fab 208*. Oldham saw the folly of their ways and took them in the opposite direction. Soon they were the sartorial antidote to the Beatle smile-and-suit look.)

The Beatles had arrived in a London dominated by Mod fashion. Tony Bramwell recalls that Mod had not yet reached Liverpool and that, when they got to London, The Beatles were fascinated to see 'all these kids running round in white hipsters and cycling shirts'.

There are those keen to bestow on The Beatles the title of first British Mod band. After all, the argument runs, The Beatles dressed in mohair, listened to r'n'b music, were upwardly mobile, reached out to Europe and America for their music and clothes and never looked backwards.

However, Mark Lewisohn quickly warns off such a reading, insisting that 'You have to remember the Beatles are never one thing or another. Yes, there were Mod elements but their haircuts were never Mod, and Mods did not listen to rock 'n' roll like they did.'

In turn, Mods – true Mods, that is – ignored The Beatles. Their position was clear: The Beatles appealed to young girls, and so what if they covered r'n'b songs? Why listen to pale imitations when the original is available? In an import shop. At a very expensive price.

The Beatles cared little for such rejection. They would always grow and develop alongside youth cults but never ever within them. McCartney's previous words about 'common herds' and 'not us at all' echo down the pages.

Even so, as lovers of style, they instinctively understood Mods. Witness Macca and John defending them at a 1964 Hong Kong press conference. Asked about Mods in London wearing pink shirts and high-heeled shoes, Paul said there was nothing wrong with that, and John added, 'They've got to get away from the in-betweens, haven't they? What else can they do, you know. They're fine.'

The Beatles were forever dipping into youth cults – Teddy Boys, Rockers, Mods and later Hippies – but they never signed the acceptance forms. This stance was brilliantly articulated by Ringo during the band's performance on the TV music show *Ready Steady Go* on Friday 20 March 1964. 'Are you Mods or Rockers?' Cathy McGowan asked the drummer. 'No, we're Mockers,' he wittily replied.

Certainly The Beatles were now having a tangible effect on young British fashion. In his 1963 article entitled 'How to Form a Beat Group', *Melody Maker*'s Chris Roberts wrote of the band: 'Their influence on some groups in the area (Liverpool) is very marked. Even their clothes and hair styles have been swept up by the club crowds who wear dark polo-neck sweaters and dark clothes as a sign of hipness.'

Meanwhile *Beatles Monthly*, first published in August 1963, announced the launch of the official Beatles sweater. It was a black polo-neck number in 100% Botany wool, with a two-tone Beatle badge embroidered on it in gold and red, and it came in one size, designed to fit the widest possible range of average-size girls.

'When it comes to clothes John, Paul, George and Ringo have plenty of ideas of their own,' Millings told the world in 1964, 'especially Paul. One thing they all have in common is that they prefer their trousers without pockets, and Paul – who designs most of his own clothes – always has his trousers to fit very low at the waist.'

Even the politicians sensed something was going on. Ted Heath (later to become British Prime Minister) famously declared that the Beatles had single-handedly saved Britain's ailing corduroy industry.

If Millings's first suits for the band had been masterpieces of style and subtlety, then the next set would prove to be a fashion masterstroke.

Pierre Cardin was a famous French designer who in the late 1950s launched the collarless jacket. John claimed that he had bought one in Paris on holiday with Paul in 1961, although there is no pictorial evidence to back up this assertion. However, it has always been assumed that the band's use of this fashion item came from their Paris trip. I would venture not. Epstein said in a 1964 interview that the boys first saw the collarless jacket in Germany during their Hamburg stint.

This is backed up by Hunter Davies's official biography, which asserts that early in their relationship Astrid Kirchherr made Stu Sutcliffe a collarless jacket to wear. Mark Lewisohn reveals that when Stu started wearing this jacket, the others – ironically for an item they would forever be associated with – teased him mercilessly. 'What are you doing with mum's suit then, Stu?' they would say, referring to its likeness to the sort of top a middle-aged woman might wear.

In keeping with the nature of the band's creativity, Cardin's jacket was an inspirational device. It was not to be slavishly copied. Working mainly with McCartney, Millings came up with a jacket significantly removed from Cardin's original design. Cardin's jacket sported five buttons at the front and three patch pockets. The round-necked, collarless Beatle jacket used three pearl buttons and two pockets with braided edges, and had single-button cuffs. The matching flat-front trousers had no side-pockets.

OPPOSITE In 1961 Paul and John hitch-hiked to France, wearing bowler hats to attract passing drivers. With success now beckoning, McCartney's use of the bowler in this picture is far more light-hearted.

Epstein's dictum to the band that their stage clothes could be outlandish and unorthodox but must always remain smart is certainly fulfilled in this instance. Once again no other band looked like The Beatles. Once again they were leading the pack. These landmark suits also operated at another level – they were androgynous, able to appeal comfortably to both sexes. At the time young men's fashion was being heavily feminised, particularly by the designer John Stephen in Carnaby Street. Although some now sneer at his work, it was Stephen and his ilk – Cecil Gee was another – that were bringing colour and style to young men's clothes, edging them ever closer to a female and indeed classless style.

As James Slaver would soon write in *Town* magazine: 'The long reign of gentility is over. What kept men's clothes formal for over a century was the idea that there was something caddish in any departure from a very rigid norm. This restriction seems to have been overcome. A man no longer feels it is necessary to show his social caste by his clothes. The way is open to every kind of innovation and we are on the brink of some startling changes.'

The Beatles' famous collarless jackets perfectly chimed with the fashion zeitgeist of androgyny, even though it was being worn by four men brought up in a highly male environment. But then that was the past, and The Beatles always looked to the future. Their clothes said as much to the world.

What is of further interest where the collarless suits are concerned is that when the band toured America, they left them behind. American audiences only got to see the band in these landmark clothes through record sleeves or magazine pictures.

Why did the band not style them for the Americans? They had first worn them in November 1963. It was now February 1964, and three months is a long time in terms of Beatle creativity. Perhaps they had just got bored of them. Other bands were now copying them and, as Mark Lewisohn states, 'Once someone copied what they were doing, they dropped it instantly and looked for something new.' Maybe they also sensed that the suits would be too provocative for the American youth.

After all, many American males sneered at The Beatles. The band wore long hair and pretty suits. American fashion was much more masculine, based on jeans,

Chino trousers, Bass Weejun shoes, button-down shirts and Harrington-style jackets. This was the All-American preppy look, and no way was a bunch of prissy Brits going to change that which was sacred in the USA.

Christopher Makris was brought up in Concord, New Hampshire. His father ran a clothes shop. Christopher became a huge Beatles fan and for months urged his dad to import Beatle-style clothing. When his father finally ordered some, Christopher was overjoyed. 'But I only wore my Beatle jacket to church on Sundays,' he tells me. 'I would not dare go to school looking like a Beatle because I would have been beaten up by my classmates, simple as that, man.' He adds that, 'We watched them all the time, but by the time we had caught up with them fashion-wise, they were already five years ahead of us.'

This chimes in with Jonathan Gould's assertion in his Beatle book *Can't Buy Me Love* that the Beatles bought Mod to America. ('Mod' in American terms has a much wider meaning than in the UK.) What Gould means is that The Beatles' relaxed and colourful style helped to pave the way for UK fashion designers. Because of The Beatles – and no one else – England, and London in particular, became fashionable in the USA. Groups such as the Dave Clark Five and Gerry and the Pacemakers benefited enormously from the Beatles' success in America, and so did fashion people. It is hard to think of any group today making such an impact. The 'London look' never took America by storm, but it was certainly hip in fashionable American circles. John Stephen opened a shop in Minneapolis, of all places, while Mary Quant and fellow London designer Caroline Charles were also welcome in the USA.

'England has become the centre for pop music, pop art, and now pop fashion. It's so exciting', Quant enthused in *Fab 208* in November 1964. 'In New Orleans, which I visited, our clothes knocked them cold. In the night clubs all the singers are imitating the Beatles. ... And the girls are wearing imported from Britain fashions.'

OPPOSITE In Liverpool, American jeans were easy to come by, thanks to local sailors returning from New York. Here John wears a pair in 1963. Indeed the only advertising campaign the band ever undertook was for a local jeans company called Libro.

Caroline Charles told *Fab 208*, 'I didn't have to sell my clothes in New York. They practically walked into the stores. Everyone loved them from the start.'

(Incidentally, Caroline's work would catch the eye of Ringo, who ordered six handmade pre-wedding suits from her. Although she was unavailable for comment herself, I was subsequently informed that Caroline and Ringo worked together on designing slightly Mod/Edwardian suits in Savile Row fabrics that were fitted in at the waist, with high collars and interesting pocket and button details. The smart, unusual jackets had matching drainpipe suit trousers. Like all of Caroline Charles's work, it was quiet, with quirky details, in top-quality fabrics and impeccably well made.)

This UK fashion phase, spearheaded by The Beatles, caught on in New York and a few other cities, although what the true effect of this development was can be summed up by a press conference in 1966, when the band were asked if they felt responsible for the USA Mod fashion revolution. The band all said no at the same time, and then John blithely added, 'We haven't noticed it.'

Certainly by 1965 many American bands were sprucing themselves up and, like Bob Dylan, taking to stage suits, polka-dot shirts, sunglasses and Beatle-style boots. Yet this was not a one-way street. Lennon sometimes wore a Dylan-style cap, although Mark Lewisohn states that he was not paying sartorial homage to the American singer-songwriter, whom The Beatles admired so much. Although they got into Dylan in Paris, after a French DJ slipped them a copy of Dylan's *Freewheelin'* album, John was already in possession of the cap before this event. This leather number was made for him by a Liverpool friend called Helen Anderson, and after Lennon wore it in Paris in January 1964, Dickins & Jones department store on London's Regent Street began a popular range of their own John Lennon caps.

It has to be said that, of all The Beatles, Lennon loved caps the most, sporting a huge amount of them in different shapes, sizes and materials. There was a bonus to this sartorial penchant of Lennon's. If in photos his fellow Beatles did not wear headgear, it meant that in photographs the viewer's eye would be instantly drawn to him, thus shoring up the idea of Lennon as Beatle Number 1. Which he was – for a couple more years.

ABOVE John being measured up for a suit in 1964.

RIGHT Dougie Millings, the so-called 'tailor to the stars', who, with the band's creative input, adapted the famous Pierre Cardin collarless jacket that The Beatles would popularise.

OPPOSITE AND FOLLOWING PAGES The Beatles first saw Pierre Cardin's collarless jacket in Hamburg. At first they poked fun at anyone wearing this style, but they changed their tune as the years went by. This look became unique to The Beatles, but when other bands started mimicking the style, they quickly dropped it.

Ludwig
THE
BEATLES

OPPOSITE John and Paul on *Ready Steady Go* in 1963. Their fellow guests were The Springfields.

ABOVE John looking dapper in his suit with velvet collar, and his friend Paul sporting a more relaxed look. By his own admission John spent much of his money on clothes.

FOLLOWING PAGES · LEFT Band and manager looking extremely smart and happy as their music and popularity gain momentum.

RIGHT 'Her Majesty is a pretty nice girl but she doesn't have a lot to say', Paul McCartney would sing many years from now, but here The Beatles acknowledge Her Majesty with a bit more respect after their appearance at the Royal Command Performance, Prince of Wales Theatre, London, in October 1963.

OPPOSITE Playing up to the cameras during rehearsals for their memorable Royal Command Performance, October 1963.

ABOVE The band pose with the line up for their Christmas show at Finsbury Park, London, in 1963. Behind them, Cilla Black, Billy J. Kramer and The Dakotas plus a young Rolf Harris vie for the camera's attention. Note the casual style of the band, especially McCartney in a suit and T-shirt, a daring look for the time. Lennon's use of a top hat betrays his love of a good titfer.

Such was the impact of the collarless suits that today, nearly fifty years later, they are associated only with The Beatles, never with their French creator. Millings's reward was to work with the Fabs for another three years.

'We did 500 variations for The Beatles eventually,' he recalled in a 1964 interview, 'Four in the set, and we always made spares. On some of the black velvet suits they had three or four different shades. There was always an extra for John, who either got thin or fat or split his trousers running from the theatre. The only complaint from The Beatles was that the trousers were not tight enough.'

I wonder where we have heard that complaint before. Because of the hysteria they ignited everywhere they went, activities such as clothes shopping were now denied the band. Instead, fashion people came to them or vice versa.

Beatles Monthly reported that on 24 June 1963 the band went to Hungarian-born shirt-maker Katy Stevens on London's Archer Street to place orders for a forthcoming photo shoot with Dezo Hoffmann. They ordered fifty shirts at £2 each. When they returned on 2 July to pick them up, the middle-aged Stevens wondered why there were youngsters on the street below, screaming up at her office. Lennon nonchalantly turned to her and explained. 'It's nothing. It's just because we are here.'

Another of Stevens's customers was Glenn Ludlow, who today is managing director of a bespoke shirtmakers called Sartorial Executive. He says Stevens's place was actually on Berwick Street, just two doors up from the Blue Posts pub, and that not only was her work of a very high standard but she also consistently under-priced her shirts. 'She was the best shirtmaker around for miles', according to Ludlow.

At a Glasgow show (probably on 5 October 1963) a Scottish American guy named Bob appeared backstage. Bob ran a made-to-measure shirt company named Esquires in Glasgow and offered his services to the band. Whatever they wanted he would make. He took their measurements, and soon the band were sending him their design requests. Make the collar longer, higher etc.

Rave magazine later reported in July 1964 that, prior to their Australian and American tour, the band ordered forty-five shirts from Esquires at a price of £156.

Rave and *Fab 208* would be instrumental in maintaining Beatlemania, and the band recognised this. Keith Altham, who wrote for *Fab 208*, reveals that the band included them in their manic work schedules. 'They would come to our Kingsway studios,' he tells me, 'and spend the afternoon having their photo taken. They knew how important the magazine was for them.'

Fab 208 was launched in January 1964. The Beatles were the cover stars of the first two issues. In edition number 1 they appear in their collarless jackets and white shirts and ties, and all smiles. Interestingly, inside there is a photo of one of Brian Epstein's other bands, Gerry and the Pacemakers. They too wear collarless jackets. The Pacemakers were one of The Beatles' first real rivals, and you can almost hear The Beatles' teeth grinding as they gaze upon that particular pic.

In the February edition the magazine ran an advert for a Beatle-inspired corduroy jacket. There were also worsted skirts to match Lennon's worsted jacket. The magazine called the girls modelling these items 'Beat Babes'.

Meanwhile *Rave* magazine was pitching the Beatles look to its mainly male audience. In July 1964 it told its readers that 'Beatle Boy people go for short jackets with two or four pleats behind, preferably a polo-neck sweater beneath. Then plain drainpipe trousers with suede boots side-zipped. The Beatles show clothes come from Dougie Millings (£30 – £40), shirts by Esquires of Glasgow, shoes by Anello and Davide.'

Paul McCartney's love of fashion design – and of grabbing a bargain – can be seen in DJ Alan Freeman's *Rave* interview with him in 1964. Halfway through the interview the band's driver, Bill Corbett, arrives with boxes of handmade shirts from Katy Stevens.

'He took out one shirt after another, all very sharp. A white one with a black velvet collar, a few in deep reds and blues with the latest big buttons, three open-weave casuals tailored in sackcloth and silk. ... Paul's a keen eye for the price too. What he paid to have that gear made up would make some big clothing names blink. It was less than half what you would expect to shell out in a good shop. Paul winked. "I got two Hungarians down the West End to make all my stuff. A little upstairs place. Only a few of us know it."'

Naturally, many have wondered if The Beatles ever used Carnaby Street. According to Tony Bramwell, they did, but only late at night, when the street was deserted. These nocturnal visits would take place after the band had visited Brian Epstein's office in nearby Argyll Street. They would wait for the streets to clear and then, under cover of dark, make the short walk to Carnaby Street and window-shop, pointing out to Bramwell items that caught their eye. The next day Bramwell would return and buy up what had been selected.

The men's fashion evolution was in full swing by now, and London was full of shops they could use: Paul's Boutique, Topper Man, His Clothes, Gentry Male, Adam, Take Six, Austin Reed, Hem and Fringe, Donis, Poco, Sportique, Trecamp Village, Mister Carnaby, You And I.

It was a great time for fashion innovation, and it would not be long before The Beatles again caught the nation's eye. On 20 April 1965 they appeared at the *NME* Pollwinners concert in Wembley wearing military-style jackets with epaulettes and a small upward-turned collar. 'That was George Harrison's idea', Bramwell reveals. 'He adapted the original Cardin jacket to have a little collar which was called a gillie collar. It was like a Nehru style.'

George often directed the Beatle look, and sometimes to an amusing end. He once recalled: 'We had seen this cloak while we were in Amsterdam. They took us down the canals for a tour and there was a guy standing on the edge with a groovy cloak on, so we sent our trusty roadie Mal Evans to find out where he got the cloak from. And about three hours later Mal arrived back at the hotel with the cloak. He'd bought it from the guy. The next stop was Hong Kong, where there was all them tailors knocking out suits and stuff for you in about ten minutes, so we all had these suits and cloaks made and we arrived in Sydney in the middle of this huge rainstorm. It was suggested we drive round on the back of a truck to wave to the fans because they'd been up all night waiting and by the time we got back to the hotel, the cloaks were, like, just, chuck them away. They had shrunk, they were dropping apart; the fabric was, like, real cheap.'

The military-style jackets would be popularised by the band in their second feature film, *Help*. Some of the suits for the film were made by Millings, while Julie Harris, who had worked with the band on their first film, *A Hard Day's Night*, was again costume designer. Harris would win an Oscar the following year for her work on the famous John Schlesinger film *Darling*. For *Help* she would be nominated for a BAFTA, but one senses that, where The Beatles were concerned, not too much work was involved.

In an interview, she recalled: 'I liked The Beatles films *Help!* and *A Hard Day's Night*. They were great. It was so exciting to be working with them. It was great to be on set when they were doing their numbers. It was wonderful.'

The band again wore the jackets for their most famous live show, the Shea Stadium gig on 15 August 1965, when over 50,000 people – a world record – attended. As they took to the stage, adorning their jackets were police badges.

Ringo explains: 'They were genuine Wells Fargo agent's badges. They were given to us while we were riding in a Fargo van on the way to the concert. John stuck his in the back of his cap.'

Within a year of that show, the entrepreneurs Ian Fisk and the appropriately named John Paul would open their shop I Was Lord Kitchener's Valet, specialising in antique military jackets, which would be covered in medals.

Perhaps the most symbolic concert the band would ever give was their show on 29 August 1966 at Candlestick Park in San Francisco. Sick of touring and the incredible hassle of moving round the world to a constant soundtrack of screams and demands on their time, The Beatles had decided that this would be their last ever show in front of a paying audience. And it was.

For the last time ever the band dressed in their stage suits and Beatle boots – all except for George, who opted for a pair of moccasin-type shoes. (George was the Beatle most anxious to get away from the concert stage, hence his deviation from the norm.)

This would be the last time the band appeared in uniform together, the last time they faced their adoring public on a stage. Furthermore, this symbolic concert would be held in a city about to become the centre of the new Hippie movement. Back in London the first inkling of this new wave of fashion and music was starting to be felt, and when it finally broke, The Beatles would be waiting.

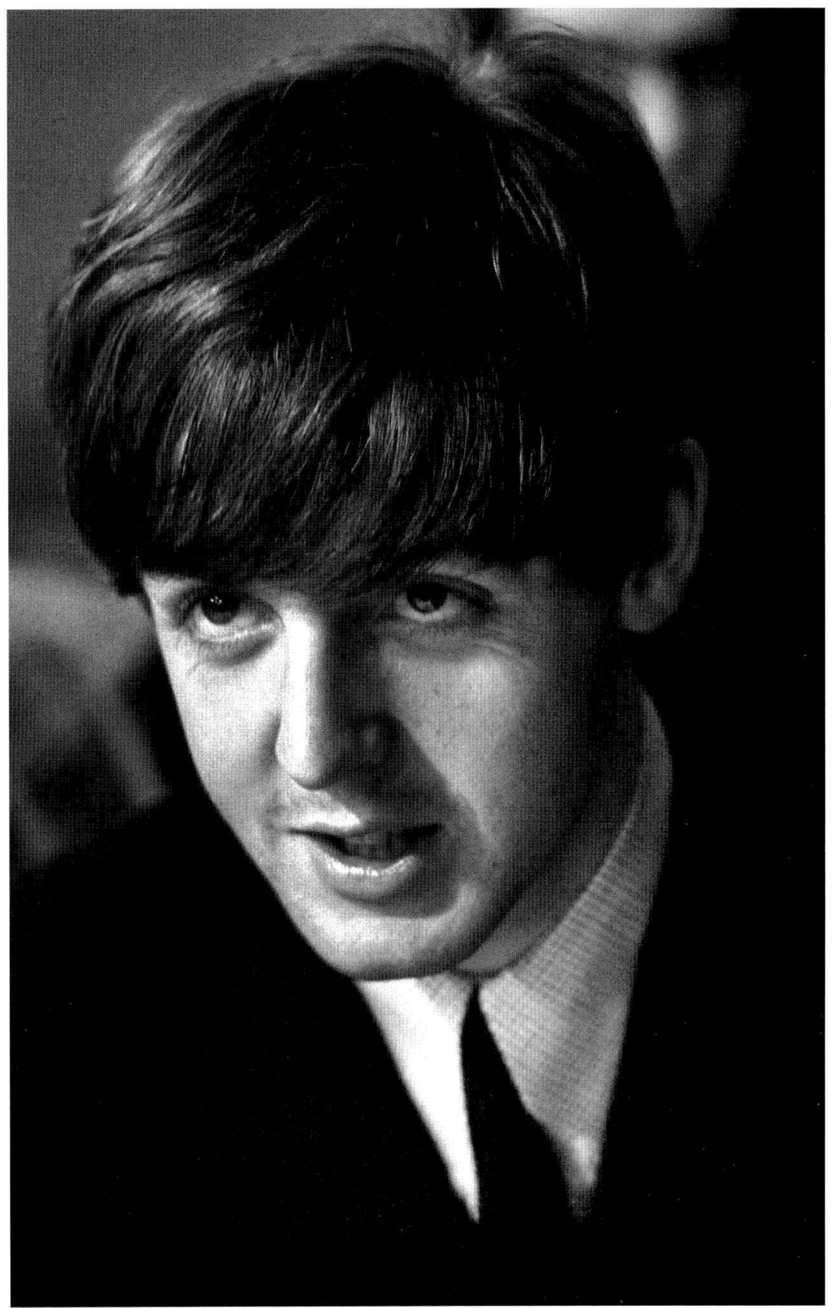

OPPOSITE A great shot of Lennon taken on 15 December 1963, while recording their appearance on *Thank Your Lucky Stars*. Note the absence of a tie and the length of John's shirt collar – very Carnaby Street.

ABOVE · LEFT TO RIGHT
Beatle stockings for sale. Apparently they cost an arm and a …
McCartney with a striking shirt collar in 1963. By now the band were designing their own shirts and having them made in London and Glasgow.

Fabulous
YEAR
KEEP YOUR DATES WITH THE
BEATLES
CALENDAR
PAUL
McCARTNEY
RINGO
STARR

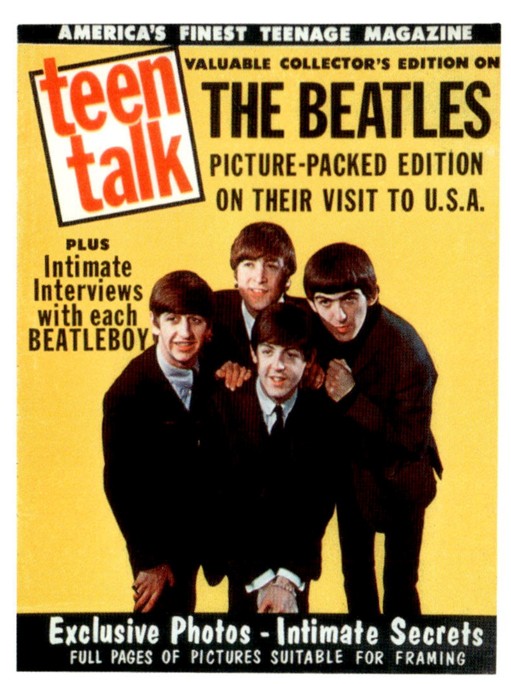

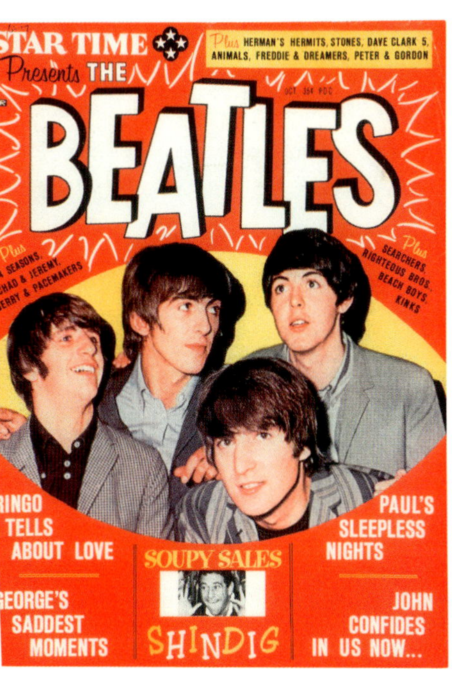

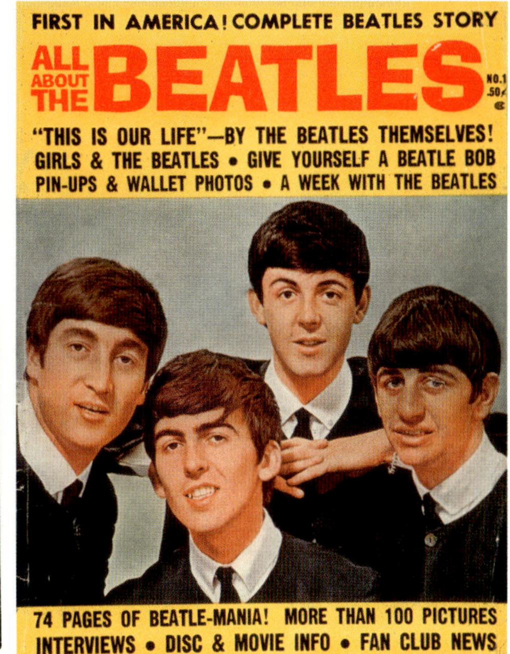

OPPOSITE Just one of the millions of fans whose lives (and bedrooms) were totally transformed by The Beatles.

ABOVE · LEFT TO RIGHT John and George signing autographs in Paris, January 1964. Lennon's use of the leather cap instantly set him apart from the rest of the band.
Four Beatle boy fans sporting the trademark Beatle style: longish hair, collarless tops and Beatle boots. Beatlemania was female-driven, but the band's music cut through all barriers.

RIGHT The band arrive in America for the first time, on 7 February 1964, to be greeted by a sea of fans. Compared with previous styles, their clothes here are downbeat and conservative, while again Lennon's use of a hat gives out the subliminal signal he wishes others to pick up on – he is the leader of this band.

OPPOSITE Brian Epstein (in trademark polka-dot scarf), Cynthia Lennon and John Lennon at London Airport, about to fly off to New York and create a sensation.

ABOVE AND OPPOSITE Images from The Beatles' sensational first tour of America. John would later say that American youth was five years behind Britain in terms of fashion.

ABOVE AND RIGHT The band back in the UK on 23 February 1964, at the ABC Television Studios in Teddington, Middlesex, recording their slot for the *Big Night Out* show.

FOLLOWING PAGES Recording their second feature film, *Help!*, in the Scala Theatre, London. The jackets both George and John wear here are defined by their unique collars, which start small and then expand. While the Mods were into three-button suits, The Beatles – of course – had to be just that little bit different and went for four.

EXIT

OPPOSITE AND ABOVE Two faces of John. In the second picture he wears a black polo-neck sweater, a clothing item he always associated with jazz fans and the Beatniks he encountered at art college.

I
LOVE
GEORGE

OPPOSITE George and Ringo looking very relaxed in shirt and jeans, while Paul sports a schoolteacher-ish look, very much in keeping with the band's power structure.

ABOVE Filming *Help!* with actor Wilfrid Brambell.

FOLLOWING PAGES · LEFT Off stage, the band dressed similarly. Note George and Ringo both in dark polo-neck sweaters and Ringo and John in almost identical suits. If someone bought a striking clothing item, the rest of the band would rush out and buy a similar number.

RIGHT John looking very Dylanesque with his cap, jeans and acoustic guitar. It was Dylan who influenced Lennon and McCartney to experiment musically and lyrically. He was also the first man to introduce them to marijuana. Perhaps this is why John looks so happy here ...

OPPOSITE Paul McCartney in classic pose, wearing quite dowdy clothing compared with his band mates.

RIGHT AND BELOW Ringo dressing in a very Mod style, with his three-button suit and button-down polka-dot shirt. John, meanwhile, is sporting the look that Van Morrison would later appropriate. Their casual clothing is in contrast to the picture above, where the band arrive in America for their second tour, again dressed quite formally.

FOLLOWING PAGES - LEFT The Beatles rehearse for the *Thank Your Lucky Stars* TV show in March 1965. Despite the band's huge success, no way would George have been allowed in front of the cameras in such casual clothing.

RIGHT The Beatles at the London Palladium in February 1965 – one of the earliest known photos of the McCartney classic thumbs-up pose. Note John's very stylish jacket. He was going through a fat period and sometimes using dark-coloured tops to cover up his stomach.

ABOVE · LEFT Brian Epstein, outside the Saville Theatre on London's Shaftesbury Avenue, where he staged his famous *Sunday at the Saville* shows.

ABOVE · RIGHT John and Cynthia off on their travels in May 1965, with John still persisting with a hat that clearly doesn't suit him.

OPPOSITE The boys filming *Help!* at Cliveden House, wearing the kind of casual clothing they would use for the sleeve of their sixth album, *Rubber Soul* – all suede jackets and long hair.

FOLLOWING PAGES · LEFT Ringo contracted tonsillitis, so Georgie Fame's drummer, Jimmy Nicol, stepped in for the band's tour of Europe and Australia in 1964. In the Netherlands, George spotted a man wearing a cape. In Hong Kong, the band had capes made up from the original design, and by the time they reached Australia all four were all wearing them. Unfortunately, torrential rain damaged them irreparably.

RIGHT On 26 October 1965 the Queen awarded each of The Beatles the MBE. 'We will have to get some Mod clothes if we are going to see the Queen', Lennon remarked before the ceremony.

O·A·C
B·O·A·C
B·O·A·C
B·O·A·C

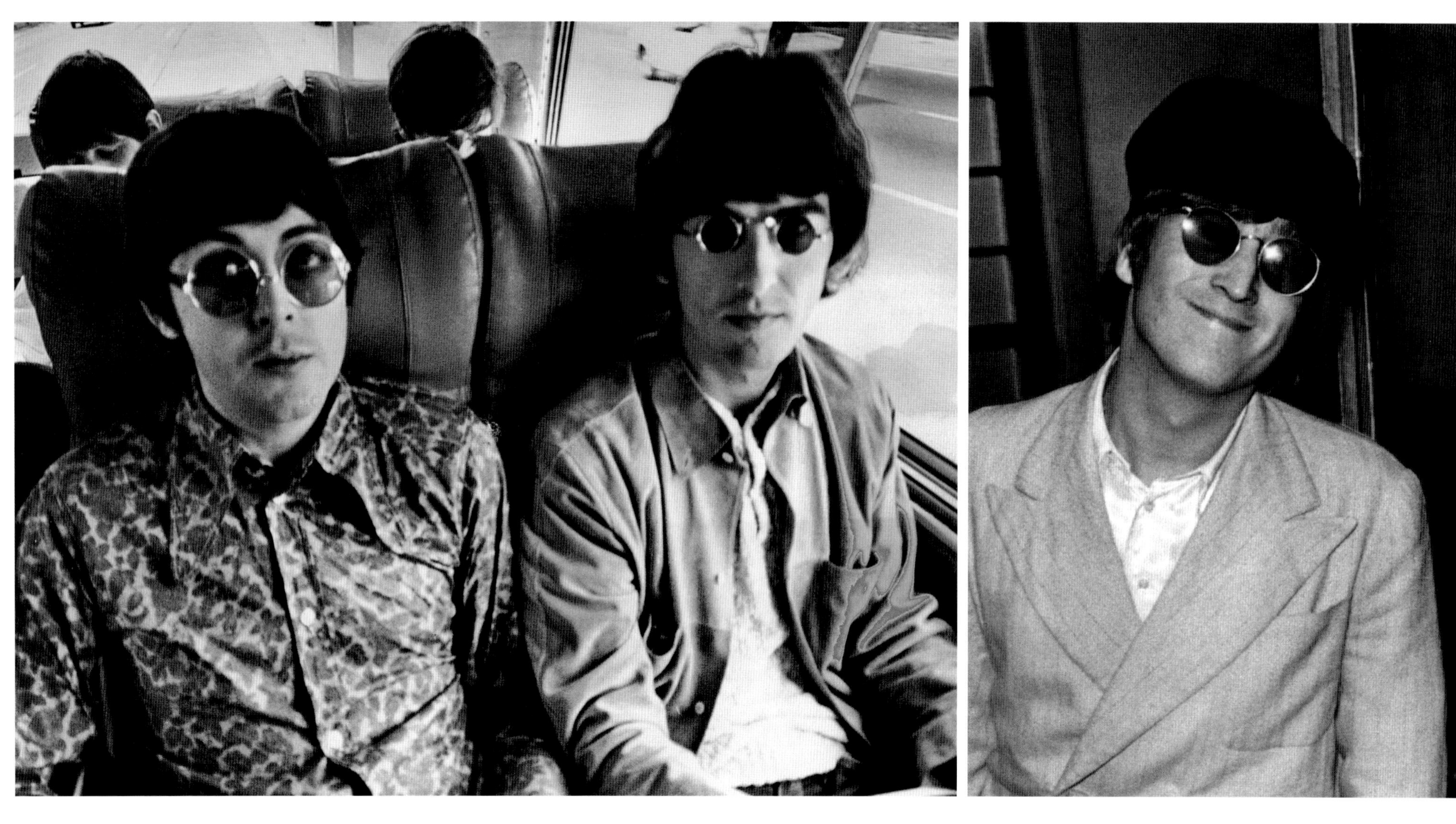

PRECEDING PAGES, ABOVE AND OPPOSITE The band were one of the first to start wearing sun-glasses as everyday wear, thus increasing their mystique as pop stars.

ABOVE AND OPPOSITE The band wore suits on stage throughout their career, but for the many press conferences they had to attend they presented themselves to the world in different styles. Note the increased use of colour in their clothes in this photograph of the band in Japan in 1966. As their music grew more interesting, so did their clothes.

FOLLOWING PAGES George seems to have caught John's penchant for choosing the wrong hat ...

OPPOSITE Brian Epstein with his boys adopting a more casual style as the party arrive back from a torrid time touring the Philippines in the summer of 1966. The jollity of Ringo's candy-striped jacket and the band's large smiles hide the tension that was now creeping into their attitude to touring. Note also John's psychedelic-inspired shirt, probably bought from the King's Road, the new centre for London fashion.

ABOVE The boys at a press conference in New York in August 1966. Their huge success created such a demand for all things British that UK designers such as Mary Quant, John Stephen and Caroline Charles were able to make great headway in the USA.

ABOVE · LEFT The Beatles, again displaying their wide range of fashion tastes, pose before the press in Los Angeles in August 1966. The world doesn't know it yet, but they have just two concerts left to play.

RIGHT Lennon arriving back in London wearing sun-glasses and a striped jacket that pays homage to the Edwardian look now gathering pace in the UK.

OPPOSITE Now you know why they call me Ringo … In fact, the drummer's nickname originated from his love of cowboys. Note also his highly stylish jacket and constant love of polka-dot shirts. Ringo was not only the best Beatles drummer in the world, but he also certainly knew how to keep up with, and then surpass, his band mates on the fashion front.

OPPOSITE John and Cynthia at home, with John still persisting with the bad hats …

LEFT The tunic worn by John for a *Time Life* magazine spread from 1966, with an estimated auction price of £30,000. The band were now deeply immersed in the King's Road style of military jackets and psychedelic clothing.

ABOVE Beatle disciple Paul Weller, of The Jam, paying tribute to the Fabs with his own recreation of their velvet-collared jacket.

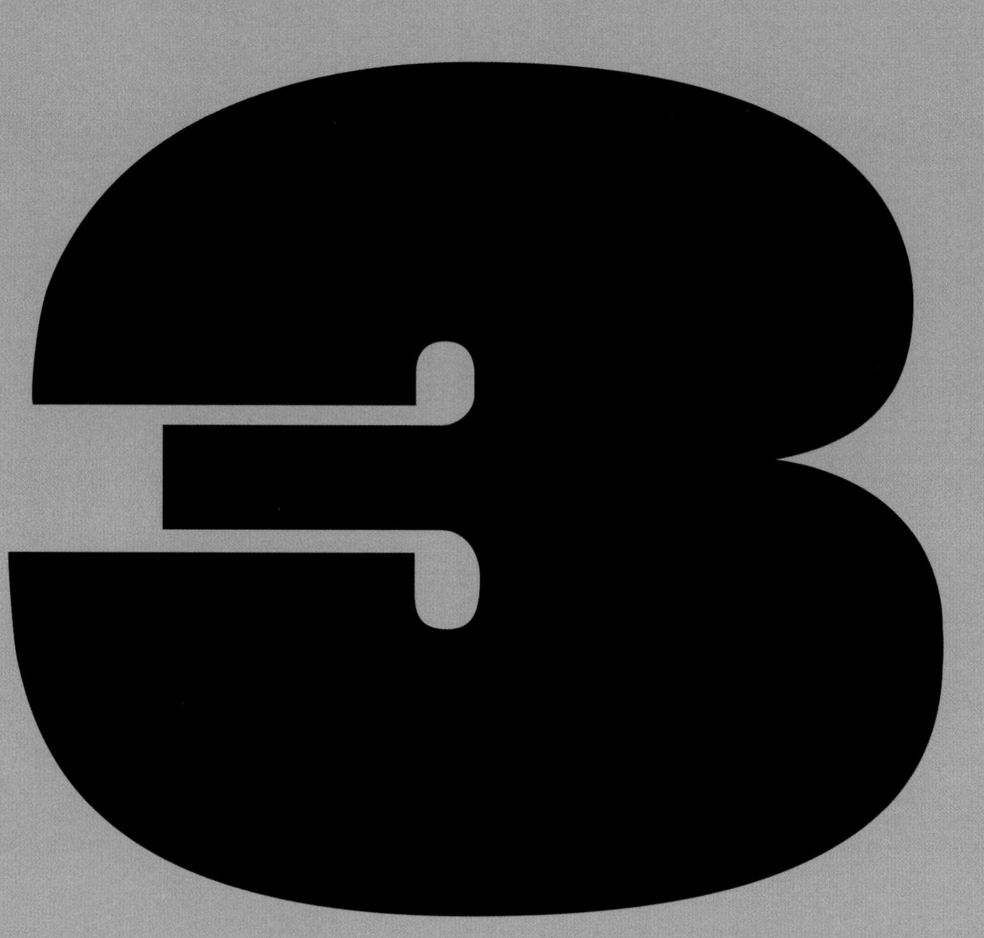

ADVENTURES IN PEPPERLAND
Chapter Three

I suppose the fashion thing was a kind of an eruption. We were erupting anyway, as The Beatles; and it is very difficult to separate the Beatles eruption from the fashion or the cultural or the mind eruption. It was all happening at once, as a whirlpool.

PAUL McCARTNEY

From a very early age Paul McCartney loved disguising himself. When he was twelve, he played a juror in a school play. His schoolmate Iain Taylor recalls McCartney's singular behaviour at this time: 'Paul would endlessly change his make-up from night to night. Since we were playing different jurors, he was able to do this. He would come up with a new look every night.'

Throughout his life Macca has loved the subterfuge that clothes offer. During Beatlemania, much to his delight, he and the band often had to disguise themselves in order to hide from hysterical fans.

At Doncaster, in 1963, the band entered the concert hall pretending to be newspaper boys in a van. In Bournemouth (again in 1963) a beard was made available to any band member wishing to leave the hotel. 'We loved dressing up', Ringo once remarked, and he was right. For photo shoots The Beatles became matadors, spies, Eskimos, policemen and cowboys.

But it was Macca who loved dressing up the most. On a brief two-day tour of Sweden in 1964 he swept back his hair, put on a moustache and some glasses, grabbed a camera and went to George's room. When his friend opened the door, Macca asked to take photos of him. The unsuspecting George told him to piss off. Macca was delighted. The next day he put on the same disguise and joined the press pack gathered downstairs, who had been told McCartney could not be present as he was ill. He began taking photos of the three remaining Beatles. No one twigged the identity of this new addition to the media scrum.

Sometimes he was rumbled, though. In Liverpool, on a day off, Macca dressed himself in a beret, some glasses and an old raincoat. He went out on a scooter and stopped for petrol ... and was instantly recognised.

Perhaps the funniest event was the *NME* Pollwinners concert at the Empire Pool, Wembley, on 1 May 1966 – the band's last ever UK show. Waiting for them at the back door was the *NME*'s Derek Johnson.

OPPOSITE Paul McCartney relaxing at Brian Epstein's house in Belgravia, London, as the band launch their classic *Sgt Pepper* album on 19 May 1967. The London stylist Julian Carr thinks Macca's use of the scarf may well have been influenced by Steve Marriott, of the Small Faces.

'I was waiting ... where the kitchens are, when this big van drew up,' he recalls, 'and four chefs got out with the proper white hats and aprons and trays of goodies in their hands. As they walked towards me, I realised it was The Beatles. They frequently adopted disguises to avoid being mobbed by screaming girls. They got in without being spotted and were running across the kitchen when Ringo tripped and his tray of cakes went everywhere, followed by the other three landing in a heap on top of him like a Marx Brothers routine. It was an awful mess, but they were so pleased to have got in with no trouble that they all thought it was just hilariously funny.'

Macca loved the idea of being able to move among people unrecognised, and it was this penchant for concealment that led to the idea behind the band's most famous album. When McCartney wrote a song called 'Sergeant Pepper's Lonely Hearts Club Band', it inspired him to take the song's sentiments much further and to disguise himself and the other group members as a new band, thus liberating them from being The Beatles.

The others had no problem with the concept, which in itself showed a new sensibility driving The Beatles forward. Freed from their so-called 'Mop-Top' image (the sobriquet given to the band by the national press), the band were eager to explore all avenues of expression. They had all taken LSD, and the drug had an influence on their music, their outlook and their clothes.

Soon John and Paul would be on TV discussing the merits of the drug, while George would be talking to the nation about the three states of consciousness – waking, sleeping and dreaming. The Four-Headed Monster was rapidly changing its spots, and its clothes.

The July 1966 edition of *Beatles Monthly* magazine gave the first clues to their new direction. 'The Beatles have discarded their black silk stage suits and fawn army jackets for a completely new and different stage attire', it announced. 'Gone too is D. [Dougie] Millings, who has been making suits for them ever since they could first afford a suit, and in comes a brand new boutique called Hung On You, which is frequented by many trend-setting pop stars. Unlike their previous uniforms, the boys have had each suit made to their own individual tastes, so the new outfits are not identical.'

Neil Aspinall, the band's road manager, described these suits in a diary he was asked to write in 1966 for *Fab 208* magazine: 'When we left for Munich at the beginning of the Germany and Far East tour on June 23rd of this year, there was no need for any decision-taking on the subject of clothes. The boys had just taken delivery of two entirely new outfits made by one of London's newer boutiques, Hung On You.

'One set of suits had big round cord finish buttons and shiny lapels. Those were in dark green. The others were in a very light grey, with thin orange stripes running down them.

'To go with the new gear the boys chose an assortment of new shirts in a cool crepe finish. No ties this trip. The shirts were orange, yellow-striped, straw and maroon – colours which seemed to be suitably interchangeable with either set of suits.' (Incidentally, when the band arrived in Munich, knowing fans gave them leather trousers and beer mugs as mementos of their now very distant German past.)

Granny Takes A Trip, Dandie Fashions and Hung On You – The Beatles had taken to these exclusive, expensive shops, all located in and around the King's Road in the London district of Chelsea. They loved the fact that they could shop in interesting locations, examine interesting clothes and meet like-minded people – all without the usual attendant hassle.

Many in the limelight felt the same way. The King's Road was rapidly usurping Carnaby Street's position as London's leading fashion centre. It was a matter of class and style. John Stephen, the man who invented Carnaby Street, was a Scottish working-class lad from the Glasgow suburb of Govan, and his clothes were stylish, mod and functional. In drug terms, he was amphetamine.

The King's Road was driven by young, upper-class misfits such as the dandy businessmen Christopher Gibbs and Michael Rainey. It was the latter who, in 1965, opened Hung On You, one of the area's first boutiques. The shop's forte was promoting imaginative clothing that sought to test all boundaries. In drug terms, Gibbs and Rainey were LSD. And so The Beatles' new artistic sensibilities chimed perfectly with theirs.

The colourful, way-out clothes these shops were creating perfectly matched the colourful, way-out sounds The Beatles were dreaming of. A synthesis of music, fashion and attitude was coming together, and it would be the band's *Sgt Pepper* album that would best capture this zeitgeist.

The Edwardian look and the Dandy style were the prominent fashions in this part of town, and The Beatles would delightfully play with both during 1966 and 1967.

Beau Brummell is the man credited with inventing Dandyism. His Number 1 rule was that the Dandy should pass unnoticed by others. But the King's Road – and The Beatles – ignored that rule. Their Dandyism was bright and colourful and psychedelic and very noticeable to all, especially in a London still dominated by conventional clothing.

Dandyism brought a Regency look to London streets. One of the proponents of this look was Michael Rainey's Hung On You shop. Rainey was married to Jane Ormsby-Gore, the daughter of Lord Harlech.

'My contribution to Hung On You was purely talking and discussing things at home', Jane told an audience when interviewed at the V & A Museum in 2006. 'We were very influenced by Byron ... those Byron shirts with frilly fronts and big sleeves. And literature: Spenser's *Faerie Queene* ... that sort of mood, rather romantic. He [Michael] would find ... lovely materials, all made in London in the East End by proper old-fashioned tailors. Everything beautifully made. He was a great stickler. The Stones and The Beatles would come in and say, "We want four of those ..."'

As for the Edwardian craze, according to *Fab 208* in 1964, that year saw the start of 'the craze for Edwardian fashions ... sleeves are straight down, fluting out at the cuffs or end in a deep ruffle or lace frill'.

OPPOSITE · ABOVE Lennon, close friend Georgie Fame and McCartney at a fancy dress party at the Cromwellian Club, London, in early 1967 to celebrate the twenty-first birthday of Fame's girlfriend, Carmen Jimenez.

BELOW McCartney in the summer of 1967, in a kimono probably given to him on the band's tour of Japan the previous year.

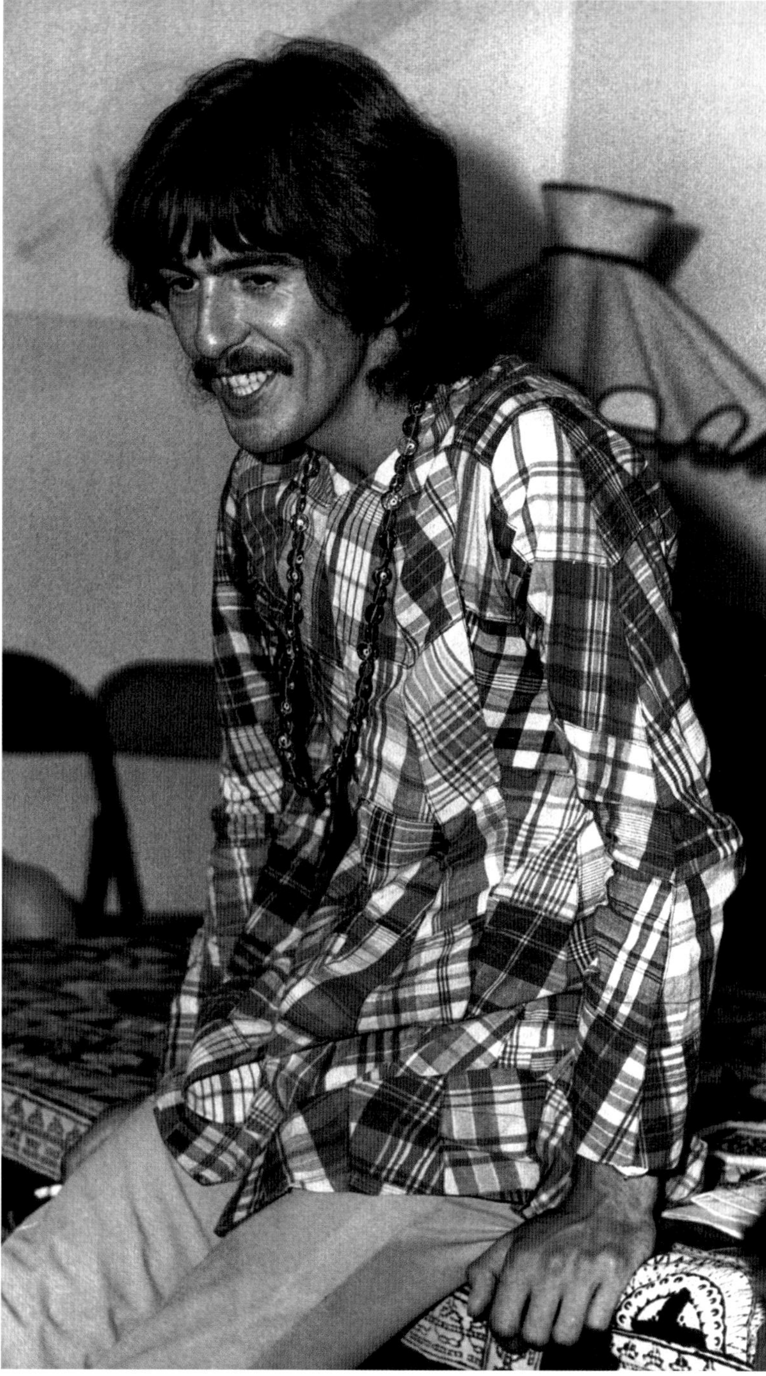

ABOVE George Harrison with the Indian musician Ravi Shankar, who influenced him enormously. It was on Ravi's suggestion that George grow a moustache to lessen the chances of being recognised in India when he went to study the sitar under him. George's collarless and colourful shirt has distinct overtones of Indian fashion.

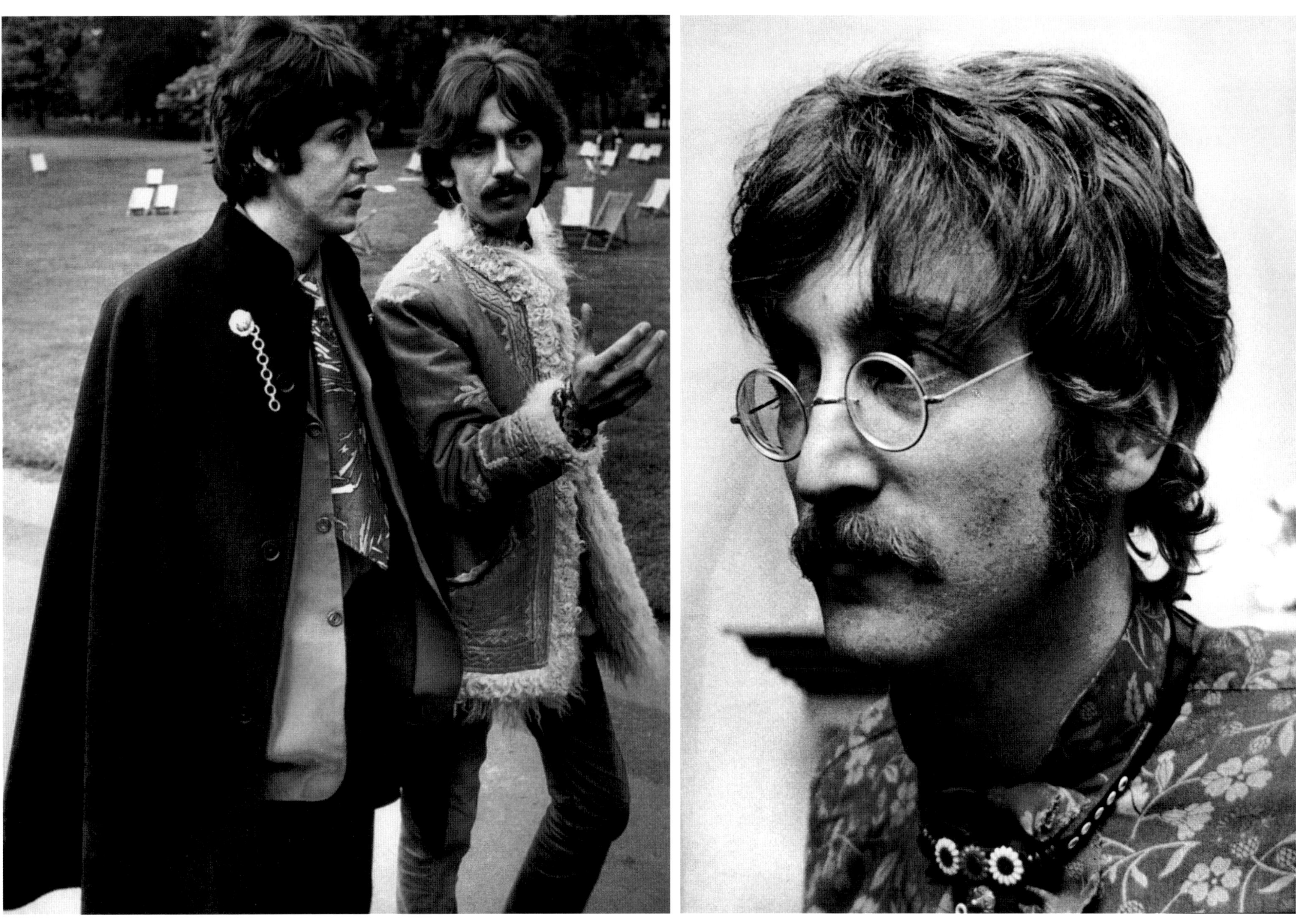

ABOVE · LEFT TO RIGHT Macca in a cloak and Harrison in an Afghan coat take a stroll in a London park in May 1967. The band's ability to take underground fashions and make them popular is evidenced here.
John Lennon sporting the King's Road look at the *Sgt Pepper* launch.

However, the magazine had not taken into account great Londoners such as the dressmaker Bunny Roger, who was already on to the style in the 1950s. Roger was a true stylist. He had worn pink shirts in the '30s, and when called up for National Service he turned his army trousers into ballet tights. It was after the war that he went Edwardian, wearing brightly coloured suits with patterned waistcoats and vital accessories such as curly-brimmed bowler hats, monocles, watch chains and gold-topped canes.

Pictures of Bunny Roger reveal a sensationally smart man but always clean-shaven, and that takes you off the scent because one of the main symbols of the male Edwardian era was the moustache, either above the lip or flowing down either side of the mouth.

McCartney was the first Beatle to wear a moustache, and he did so out of necessity. According to Tony Bramwell, the day before the shoot for 'Paperback Writer' and 'Rain', McCartney fell off his moped and badly cut his lip. Not so, says Mark Lewisohn: Macca had fallen off his moped months before. The day before the shoot, he was having his tooth crowned. In front of the cameras, chewing gum and make-up covered up the wound. 'So I started to grow a moustache – a sort of Sancho Panza thing – mainly to cover where my lip had been sewn. It caught on with the guys in the group: if one of us did something like growing his hair long and we liked the idea, we'd all tend to do it. And then it became seen as a revolutionary idea, that young men of our age should definitely grow a moustache. And it all fell in with the Sgt Pepper thing, because he had a droopy moustache ... John had a moustache cup. It had a little hole underneath the lip so you could drink tea from it without getting your moustache in it – rather fetching.'

George claimed he grew his for different reasons.

'Moustaches were part of the synchronicity and the collective consciousness', he recalled. 'What happened to me was that Ravi Shankar wrote to me before I went out to Bombay [in 1966] and in the letter said try to disguise yourself – "Couldn't you grow a moustache?" Not that it's going to disguise me but I have never had a moustache before, so I'll grow it.'

At that time, says The Beatles' hairdresser, Leslie Cavendish, only two kinds of people wore moustaches: spivs and old people. For The Beatles to adopt them speaks volumes about their imagination and style. 'As soon as they started wearing them,' Cavendish recalls, 'you saw loads of people out on the street with moustaches.'

These moustaches also imbued the band with a trendy Edwardian look, which they then wore into shops such as the increasingly hip outlet Dandie Fashions. Who first alerted them to these new shops has yet to be revealed. However, the Rolling Stones were very early proponents of the King's Road look, and it is a good bet that Brian Jones, the Stones' best dresser, told his Beatle mates about this exciting new fashion development. Jones would always catch the band's attention through his clothing. Good dressers forever circle each other with great interest.

Dandie Fashions was opened up by an Australian named John Crittle. Crittle – the father of the ballet dancer Darcey Bussell – was a great innovator whose star was on the rise in the mid-'60s.

'The Rolling Stones, Georgie Fame, Paul Getty Jnr, Brigitte Bardot, Françoise Hardy and Twiggy's manager, Justin de Villeneuve, are among the pop jet set who are wearing dandy fashions', *Fab 208* reported in December 1966. 'And they all go to an out-of-the-way boutique called Dandie Fashions in Kensington Mews. The clothes are designed by John Crittle and his wife, Andrea, and they are now going to open a new shop in the King's Road, Chelsea.'

Ringo and George were most taken by the Dandy look. Ringo in particular spent a lot of time in very sharp suits with interesting collars and cuffs, set off by shirts with ruffled fronts. The London stylist Julian Carr thinks Ringo – and George – great Dandies of their time, and he is not wrong. John and Paul headed more for the Edwardian style, seeking out stripy ties, brightly coloured jackets and the appropriate facial hair.

OPPOSITE The classic *Sgt Pepper* album sleeve, designed by artist Peter Blake and the first to be in full colour and to carry lyrics. The band's uniforms were hired from the theatrical outfitters Bermans, and the photograph was taken in a studio just off the King's Road by photographer Michael Cooper.

STEREO

The Beatles were very impressed with Crittle's clothes and kept him in mind for a business project they were starting to think about, a project they would call Apple. Their other favoured shop for clothes was Granny Takes A Trip, owned by Nigel Waymouth, Sheila Cohen and John Pearse.

Pearse was the shop's clothes designer, and his career neatly symbolises the relocation of London fashion from the West End to the King's Road. In the early '60s he landed a Soho tailoring job. In 1965 he upped sticks for the King's Road and the shop Granny Takes A Trip.

'My two partners were significant as well', he tells me in his shop in Meard Street, Soho. 'Waymouth was very much influenced by Aubrey Beardsley at that time, and the old clothes, which would have been Victorian ... re-jigging.' (Beardsley was an English artist of the late nineteenth century, famous for his distinctive erotic and decadent pictures, drawn in black ink.)

Pearse agrees that all this playing around with military uniforms from the days of the British Empire was to do with satire, attacking the still prevalent notion of Britain as a mighty world power, subjugating others at will.

He also tells me that, yes, he took LSD, and yes, it affected his creations. 'Purple came into it a lot – that was certainly drug-influenced – and rainbow patterns and swirly ... I think it did suit the Art Nouveau. God forbid I'd want to take it any more but the street, the puddles, was like really full-on groovy ...' And then one day he looked up and The Beatles were knocking at his door.

'I remember the first day they rocked up – John and Paul – and they were really impressed with the décor. We had done it all ourselves. This was '66. I was only eighteen, seventeen, Nigel [Waymouth] was a bit older, it was quite significant that in our age bracket we could take a shop and make it happen. Yeah, they came and started buying stuff, and then George turned up. I have a good iconic shot of him in a flowered jacket that we used to make. And they were no longer touring then, they were making *Sgt Pepper* and *Revolver*.'

My brain clicks the *Revolver* album cover into view. 'Must be John's', I tell him.

'Probably. I've got a good shot of Syd Barrett wearing one. He used to have a ruffle and a Liberty print. And we were financing these trips to Kabul to get Afghan coats – they had a lot of that stuff. I remember John walking around in an Afghan stinking things out. And we used to make trousers with flower prints. They would probably have two of everything. The road manager would come down and stock up, Henry Doran I think his name was [Terry, actually]. He'd come down and say, "What have you got for the boys?"'

For once The Beatles could browse and hang out with like-minded people – the groovy set, no less – and buy some shirts ... or maybe not. It didn't matter. All The Beatles knew is that after years of experiencing public hysteria, these small, delightfully decorated shops offered an oasis of tranquillity.

Occasionally there would be the odd encounter, though.

'Salman Rushdie lived upstairs', Pearse tells me. 'I remember Lennon came into the shop and Rushdie saw the Rolls outside. He scuttled down, busy trying to ingratiate himself and Sheila turned to him and said, "Don't you know conversation's dead now?" Salman actually told Nigel this story, and I think he wrote it in one of his pieces for *The Times*. But no, there was never any hysteria, and I think that's what they liked. There used to be this publication called *IT*, and John would sit here and he'd be selling it to people, encouraging people to buy it.

'And Paul was getting very interested in maybe opening a clothes shop himself. I genuinely liked them as guys, and I thought the *Sgt Pepper* album was pretty groundbreaking at the time. And it was very nice 'cause there was them and there was Mick [Jagger] and Brian [Jones]. There was camaraderie, and you'd be going to the same clubs, and Jimi Hendrix had come to town. It was a real renaissance.'

On 10 December 1966 EMI released The Beatles' first compilation album, entitled *Oldies But Goldies*. As Julian Carr points out, the cover for this album is significant. As it was an official release, the designer David Christian would have worked with the band on the cover. His colourful drawing of an archetypal Beatle is dressed in orange and yellow striped trousers, a pinkish jacket with large tie and shirt to complement his Beatle haircut. There was no reference to collarless suits, Beatle boots or anything that might connect them to the past. In fact, the sleeve brilliantly pre-dates the cartoon style that would be employed for the Beatles' fourth film, the animated cartoon *Yellow Submarine*. This psychedelic-inspired drawing could be read, then, as the band preparing their fans for the drastic change of image they would unveil in the video for their next single.

Certainly The Beatles were keeping a low profile. No more press conferences, no more informal chats – they would now put all their energies into their work. Between November 1966 and March 1967 the world saw the band on television just three times.

The first was outside Abbey Road Studios, where each member was interviewed as he entered the recording studio. The band all wear different clothes now, and the two most eye-catching sights for keen Beatle-watchers were undoubtedly George Harrison's fur coat, moustache and long hair, centre-parted and cascading well over his shoulders, and Lennon's use of the college scarf, a clothing item he would wear regularly over the subsequent winter months.

Lennon's use of the college scarf in this period is interesting. It first emerged in 1938, and its stripes echoed the Edwardian style. But I think Lennon's use is more personal. He would have seen the scarf in great numbers at his Liverpool art college in the late '50s. Given that The Beatles had just recorded 'Strawberry Fields', Lennon's groundbreaking paean to his childhood (and that *Sgt Pepper* was originally planned as a concept album, based on the band's days in Liverpool), I think the college scarf was his conduit towards a remembrance of all things past.

Certainly, clothes seem to have acted as a means of inspiration for the rest of the band, as a report in *Beatles Monthly* in 1967 suggests.

'The current Beatles recording sessions are producing some very trendy clothes as well as some forward-looking songs', it told the world. 'The variety of musical instruments in the studio is only equalled by the varying styles of the Beatles suits, jackets, ties and shoes. Paul zipped in the studio wearing a lemon-yellow jacket set off by a brightly striped tie. George strolled in with his Civil War moustache, but minus beard. A long black Mississippi gambler's jacket and black moccasins set off his moustache. Ringo and John arrived in John's Mini with blacked-out windows, of course. The new moustache and sideburns suit Ringo very much but curiously they are blacker than his medium-brown hair. So much so that people say that he's stuck them on. John's Chinaman-type moustache topped a neckerchief, held together at the throat by a badge inscribed with the words "Down With Pants".'

On Monday 30 January 1967 they took a break from recording to make two videos for their new single. Their previous video had shown the band crisp and attractive in their sunglasses, dark, sharp suits and brilliantly styled haircuts. Even the most dyed-in-the-wool Mod would have approved of the band's look.

In the videos for 'Strawberry Fields Forever' and 'Penny Lane' no such sensibility was on view. Instead, The Beatles changed tack yet again and announced to the world through their clothing and music that new horizons were now being discovered. Both films have a deliberately hallucinatory quality to them that is heightened by the band's clothing.

This included the wearing of woollen hats, flat caps, caps with badges, coats with badges, scarves, candy-striped jackets, more scarves, military jackets, striped ties, red jackets, yellow jackets, white trousers, blue shirts, patterned shirts, polo-neck jumpers, pink shirts and a red jumper – a veritable kaleidoscope of colours and styles.

Their next notable public engagement took place on 19 May at Brian Epstein's house in Belgravia, London. *Sgt Pepper* was now finished, and it was time to launch this groundbreaking album.

A handful of selected journalists were invited to Brian Epstein's house to hear the work and talk to the band. One of the guests was the DJ Kenny Everett, who would later report: 'They were dressed in the usual Beatle-type garb, consisting of a million different colours. John wore red trousers with a green shirt, which had yellow flowers leaping about all over it. No pockets in his trousers, of course, so a sporran was the natural thing to wear – well it was for him anyway.'

In the reports from this party it is Lennon's clothes that are written about the most, and that probably delighted him. And a sporran – how brilliant was that touch? He and McCartney were close friends, but they were also songwriters, and therefore self-centred and highly competitive creatures. The sporran gave Lennon the item that would draw all the attention his way. (It was also a fine place to stash things of an illegal nature.)

LEFT If the band were worried about the impact of the *Sgt Pepper* album on the British public, this joyous photo certainly conceals any anxieties they may have had.

However, according to his wife, Cynthia, when it came to buying new clothes, Lennon was a bit of a worrier. 'I always had to be his critic or his admirer when it came to the clothes he had bought for himself', she wrote in her book *John*. '"How does this look, Cyn? Does it go better with this? Do the colours look OK together? Are the trousers too baggy? What do you think, Cyn?" A trying-on session could last for hours.'

The music for their *Sgt Pepper* album was, of course, highly acclaimed, but the sleeve also drew great attention, costing, as it did, a record-breaking £2,000 or more. Presented in full colour and displaying for the first time ever the lyrics of the songs inside, it also depicted the band in silk military suits of differing colours, with a collage of famous faces behind them.

The artist responsible for the sleeve, Peter Blake, later revealed that the inspiration for this innovative sleeve came when he and McCartney walked past a Hung On You window display. Fittingly, the photo shoot for the sleeve took place at photographer Michael Cooper's studio in Flood Street, just around the corner from the King's Road.

The uniforms the band wore had been hired from a theatrical outfitters called Bermans, located on London's Shaftesbury Avenue. As *Beatles Monthly* revealed, 'Bermans sent a fellow to the recording studio with sample materials. The Beatles picked out the four brightest patterns and ordered orange and yellow patent leather shoes. The Beatles then nipped into Bermans, got themselves measured up and kitted out, sorted out the hats and that was the uniform.' For the photo shoot Paul and George pinned their MBE medals to their jackets.

In June 1967 *Sgt Pepper* was released, to wide acclaim. For many its confident and differing music styles, the innovative way it moved between psychedelia and pop and music hall, r'n'b and Indian music, summed up the spirit of the times, a period that many were calling the 'Summer of Love'. The Beatles had touched on all the elements creating that time – they had taken the drugs, taken on board the Hippie philosophy emanating from San Francisco and worn the King's Road clothing. Soon they would be in Wales meditating.

OPPOSITE A photo from early 1968 of the Dutch design team The Fool, who would play a significant part in the band's life over the next year or so.

But The Beatles did not stop there. To cap an incredible period of activity, the band gathered at Abbey Road studios on 25 June 1967 to perform their latest song, 'All You Need Is Love', to a worldwide TV audience. (The song had been written and recorded after *Sgt Pepper*, further proof of the band's incredible high-quality output.) Filmed as a party within Abbey Road studios – Mick Jagger, Keith Richards, Keith Moon and Eric Clapton were all among the guests – Lennon's message of love was relayed to billions of people worldwide, and by a band wearing clothes that were the epitome of London fashion in 1967.

Their look was smart and Hippie and King's Road and jumbled up but, above all, individual. Lennon wore a Regency-type coat with the cuffs billowing out, Macca was in a flowery shirt and slightly flared hipsters, George had opted for a dark jacket with orange trousers and Ringo wore a purple silk top. They had gone from suits and Beatle boots to a kaleidoscope of colour and style in the time it takes to hail a newspaper taxi.

Many of the clothes for the 'All You Need Is Love' session had been created by a Dutch design group that the band had got to know over the preceding few months. They were called The Fool.

The Fool's founders were a couple called Marijke Koger and Simon Posthuma. Marijke had met Simon when she was eighteen. They worked together in a gallery cum boutique in Amsterdam called The Trend, and with a third member, named Josje (or Yosha) Leeger, they produced a fashion line called Flashing Fashion.

Simon and Marijke then went travelling and ended up in Ibiza. They moved to London in 1966 and through various contacts made contact with Robert Stigwood, manager of the supergroup Cream, made up of Eric Clapton, Jack Bruce and Ginger Baker. They designed some costumes for the band and also decorated their instruments. They also worked with The Hollies on the cover of their *Evolution* album.

Shortly after this they fell in with a PR company run by Simon Hayes. Hayes had been employed by The Beatles' manager, Brian Epstein, to handle the PR for the series of concerts he was staging every Sunday at London's Saville Theatre on Shaftesbury Avenue. (The building is now a cinema.)

The Fool were now commissioned to design the concert programme for the gigs, and it was this work which allowed them to fall into Beatleworld. 'One evening Mal Evans [the Beatles' roadie] brought John and Paul to our studio in St Stephen's Gardens, where they blew their minds over the painted armoire (which was later used as part of the set design Simon and I did for the *Wonderwall* film) and our paintings and my fashion designs', writes Marijke.

'Simon Hayes also introduced us to Barry Finch, who later became a member of The Fool, as well as Ben Stagg, who later became Simon's and my personal manager. That year [1967] I asked my old school friend Yosha Leeger (a fabulous fashion designer) to come stay with us also, and so The Fool was born. The name The Fool came from my interest in the Tarot, which was introduced to me by Graham Bond, the great organ player of the Graham Bond Organisation. Yosha and I then designed costumes for Procol Harum, The Move and other bands.'

The Beatles invited The Fool to the filming of *A Day in the Life*, and George Harrison later commissioned them to paint a mural around his fireplace. Meanwhile George's wife, Pattie Boyd, happily modelled and subsequently bought some Fool clothing.

While all this was happening, though, tragedy struck. On 27 August 1967 Brian Epstein was found dead at his London home. He was just thirty-two.

According to Epstein's biographer Ray Coleman, the band had intended to dress in psychedelic clothing for his funeral, but in deference to his mother, Queenie, they wore civilian clothing.

It was probably the right move. As Ringo would point out, not all of England was enamoured of the new London fashion. 'I had a guy working for me in Weybridge,' he once revealed, 'the artist Paul Dudley, and when he was around me he had his beads on and his Afghan – but when he went back up North he put his brown suit on. A lot of Flower Power did not translate in Oldham or Bradford and not really in Liverpool.'

To get over Epstein's passing, McCartney quickly organised the making of The Beatles' third film, to be called *Magical Mystery Tour*. The idea was to put the band and several invited guests on a coach, drive randomly and film the proceedings. The Fool were asked to create some of the clothing for the film. When it was shown, on Boxing Day 1967, it was to a chorus of huge disapproval from public and critics alike.

And yet The Beatles remained hugely popular. They had been such a positive force in most people's lives that no one wanted to say goodbye to them, so they became a part of the family. Others bands knocked on your door, and you invited them in for a cup of tea and maybe a smoke, and you were captivated by them, even went out on a few occasions with them, but at some point they got boring or lost their edge or lost their way, and then you had to show them to the door and wait for the next bunch to come along. The Beatles were different; you kept a permanent space in your house for those guys. Oh, sometimes they annoyed you with some of their records or their clothes or their sayings. But in the end you always forgave them, because they were The Beatles and, be it their music or their fashion, you just knew it was going to be all right.

OPPOSITE This LP sleeve for The Beatles first compilation gave one of the first hints of the band's new style.

FOLLOWING PAGES · LEFT Down-to-earth Ringo was the smartest Beatle on show at the launch of *Sgt Pepper*, with a typically imaginative bespoke suit and tie.

RIGHT Lennon, wearing a sporran and a frilly psychedelic shirt with beads for the launch of the *Sgt Pepper* album, captures the fashion sensibility that was emanating from the King's Road. The effect of such clothing was to deepen the aura of invincibility around the band. Previously the clothes the band wore had been accessible. A Beatle fan could dress like a Beatle. But now that had all changed. The King's Road items were exclusive one-offs, out of the price range of most. The effect was to make the band even more godlike in many fans' eyes.

stereo
A COLLECTION OF BEATLES
OLDIES

OPPOSITE AND ABOVE Lennon was the most enthusiastic advocate of the drug LSD, and its influence on his clothing can clearly be seen. The Mop Tops were dead: long live *Sgt Pepper*!

BELOW The impact of the band's *Sgt Pepper* look continues to echo down the ages, as these photos of the Bee Gees, Katy Perry and Kanye West prove.

FOLLOWING PAGES · LEFT George arriving at Abbey Road in June 1967 for the historic worldwide TV transmission of the band's new song 'All You Need Is Love'. Note the candy-striped shoes. George had a thing about footwear. As a teenager in Liverpool he had explored the possibility of a corduroy shoe, much to the amusement of the local cobblers.

RIGHT Ringo goes Hippie for the 'All You Need Is Love' session, and George gives his approval.

OPPOSITE Compared with their *Sgt Pepper* phase, Paul and John calmed down a little with their clothing for the *Our World* broadcast in 1967. Ringo's outfit was made by The Fool, and, although he loved the design, he later complained that it affected his drumming. For the *One World* show every country contributed an art work in a live format; The Beatles represented the UK with 'All You Need Is Love'.

ABOVE Note John's badge, heralding the start of a new trend within the band.

FOLLOWING PAGES Never before had the band been so near the cutting edge of fashion, their clothes beautifully matching the kaleidoscope of sounds they were using in their music.

Paul McCartney and Mick Jagger, two of the biggest pop stars of the '60s (and still two of the biggest pop stars of today), travel to Bangor, Wales, to spend time meditating with the Maharishi. Note Macca's Indian-style top.

FIRST

OPPOSITE On 27 August 1967 Brian Epstein accidentally overdosed on pills and passed away. He was just thirty-two years old. His influence on the band's clothing, especially in the early days, was huge. Epstein himself rarely forsook the classic 'English gentleman' style.

ABOVE · LEFT TO RIGHT Attention to spirituality was part of the new consciousness pervading London, and of course The Beatles were the first band to explore this idea. Here, dressed in their best psychedelic gear, John and George visit the Maharishi in London. John and Paul return from a holiday in Greece, sporting the smart King's Road Hippie look.

ABOVE · LEFT TO RIGHT A typically imaginative shop façade created by Granny Takes A Trip to attract customers. Here they use half of a 1948 Dodge to create the impression that a whole car is coming out of the wall.
Two customers leaving the Granny Takes A Trip shop, situated at 488 King's Road.

OPPOSITE Flower Power invades London – a development the Beatles were very much in favour of.

OPPOSITE · LEFT TO RIGHT McCartney sporting the classic Edwardian look, all stripes and moustaches. The Edwardian craze began when charity and second-hand shops started accessing a lot of old army uniforms. It was also a good way for the young to poke fun at the dwindling British empire.
McCartney wearing a tank top made for him by his aunt and thus starting another neat fashion trend.

ABOVE Models outside the shop I Was Lord Kitchener's Valet, which specialised in military jackets, a trend the Beatles had started back in 1965, when they appeared at the *NME* Pollwinners concert.

PRECEDING PAGES, OPPOSITE, ABOVE AND RIGHT Images from *Magical Mystery Tour*, which the band started filming in September 1967. It's interesting to note that, apart from the odd Afghan coat here and striped jacket there, they seem to be heading back towards suits and a more funky traditional style.

ABOVE AND OPPOSITE The Beatles in India, February 1968. John and Paul wrote many songs while on retreat with the Maharishi. They also dressed down considerably, many of their Indian-style clothes being provided by local tailors.

FOLLOWING PAGES Ringo and George at the *Yellow Submarine* première in Piccadilly Circus, their frilly and ornate-fronted shirts turning both men into exquisite Dandies for their time.

ABOVE John, Paul and Yoko at the première of the *Yellow Submarine* film. Both Beatles hold apples, as symbols of their newly formed Apple company. John wears mainly white, a colour he took to just after leaving Cynthia for Ms Ono.

OPPOSITE The band's popularity reflected by the thousands of fans who stopped traffic, hoping to get a glimpse of their idols at the *Yellow Submarine* première.

yeah!
yeah!
the
BEATLES
T.M.
HAIR
SPRAY
yeah!
yeah!
yeah!
yeah!
© Copyright NEMS ENT. LTD. 1964
LICENSED BY SELTAEB INC.
CRYSTAL CLEAR
FINEST QUALITY
BRUSHES OUT INSTANTLY

HUR, THERE AND EVERYWHERE

Chapter Four

That bit about we changed everybody's hairstyles – something influenced us, whatever was in the air. Pinpointing who did what first doesn't work. We were part of whatever the Sixties was. It was happening itself. We were the ones chosen to represent it, what was going on on the street. It could have been somebody else but it wasn't: it was us and the Stones and people like that.

JOHN LENNON

PRESS CONFERENCE · MINNEAPOLIS · 21 AUGUST 1965

JOURNALIST *I'd like to ask you all a personal question about your hair. How can you sleep at night with it that long?*

JOHN *Well, when you're asleep, you don't notice.*

At every press conference the same question. Riots might be erupting on the streets, prominent leaders taking bullets, but still the journalists would persist: Beatles, why is your hair so long?

In a way, understandable. Beatles hair (or 'hur', as they called it in Liverpool) was groundbreaking, revolutionary; no performer in recent times had dared to wear hair at such a length. For hair to be worn on or over the collar was an affront to public decency.

It was all to do with the war. Thousands of British soldiers had arrived home wearing the army short-back-and-sides cut. In a nod to their deep heroism, the public maintained this haircut as a mark of respect.

Beatle hair went directly against this unspoken rule of British life. When people first saw it, they gasped, and so Beatle hair became as much a topic of conversation in the '60s as the Profumo scandal, the Common Market and the devaluation of the pound.

The problem with the Beatle generation was that the war meant very little to them. As Ringo once explained: 'If a house had been blown up, all it meant to us kids was that it was another place for us to go and play in.'

Because of their laissez-faire attitude towards social mores, Beatle hair paved the way for the '60s to begin. Beatle hair helped build the teenage world, helped open up a huge schism between children and parents. It created the battleground where the young and the old would slug it out for years over issues of freedom and expression. Today no one blinks at long hair. In the '60s, if you wore your hair long, you would have been considered unemployable and totally undesirable.

OPPOSITE The band would adopt many differing hairstyles over their amazing twelve-year career.

There were two reasons why The Beatles got away with their hairstyles: their public charm – even the Queen was taken with their cheeky personas – and the fact that they never waved the flag for long hair. They just wore it and let everybody else deal with it.

Furthermore, longish hair was highly attractive. Many female Beatle fans had hair of a similar length to the band and thus strongly identified with the Fabs. The band's hair said to the young girls and to rebel-minded boys, 'We are one as you are one and we are all together.'

Yet hair remained a hot issue for many years, and part of the reason was gay sexuality. Bunny Roger, the famous dandy war hero and dresser, once explained: 'If your ears didn't show, you were effeminate. It was simple, really.'

That idea was radically challenged in the early '50s, when two youth factions emerged to defy the short-back-and-sides principle.

Teddy Boys based their hairstyle on the cut worn by the American film star Tony Curtis. Curtis's hair had a curl at the front and a parting at the back, which got to be known as a 'DA'. (It resembled a duck's arse.) Teddy Boys (like Elvis, who also appropriated the style) made more of the hair at the front, brushing it upwards so as to create a quiff. John Lennon was quick to adopt the style.

'He was the first kid at Quarry Bank to boast a "Tony Curtis" hairstyle – crowned by a magnificent elephant's trunk *à la* Elvis with his sides swept back into what we called a "duck's arse"', Pete Shotton reported.

As Billy Shepherd would also report – rather breathlessly – in his book *The True Story of The Beatles*, 'There are pictures of the boys in those days. John, who now has one of the most distinctive hair-cuts in the world, then sported a weird-looking quiff, the "hur" piled up above his forehead. All the forehead could be seen. Now, of course, it is a cardinal rule that a Beatle's forehead is NEVER seen by the public.'

When Lennon met Paul McCartney at the Woolton fête, McCartney had exactly the same hairstyle. 'His hair was brushed back from the forehead and set with Brylcreem in a Tony Curtis cut', Barry Miles reported in his biography *Paul McCartney: Many Years From Now*.

ABOVE AND OPPOSITE The first significant hairstyle for the band was the Teddy Boy haircut, known as the 'DA'. The hair was swept back from the forehead and channelled into a hair tunnel at the back. The American actor Tony Curtis is credited with popularising the style in Britain. John's aunt Mimi would have been horrified by his hair in this shot, although Lennon always thought of himself as 'a weekend Teddy Boy'. George's mother was far more understanding, and told writer Hunter Davies that the length of her son's hair was nothing to do with her.

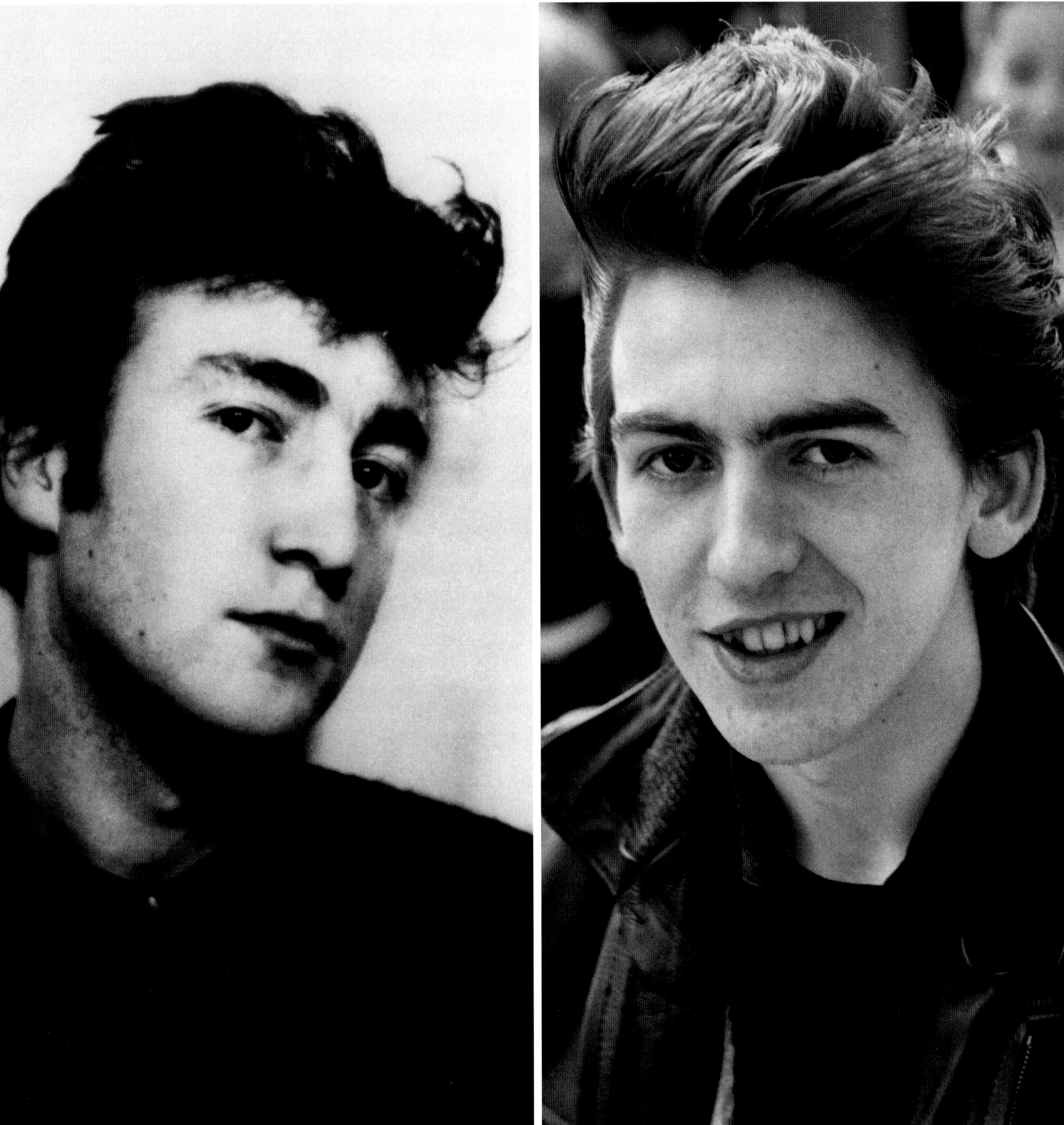

'Other haircuts of the late '50s he could have considered included the crew cut (half an inch all over), a brush cut ... a TV cut, where the hair is shaped into two bunches meeting in a V on the forehead, a style popular with the Teddy boys from Garston ... They also affected the variant jelly-roll hair, greased, combed forward and rolled to make a floppy detumescent tube hanging over the forehead, as popularised by Gene Vincent and worn ensemble with a long DA.'

All the pre-fame Beatles – George and Ringo, Stu Sutcliffe and Pete Best – wore the Teddy Boy style. In fact, it was Best's refusal to change his hairstyle that best symbolised the attitude gap between the drummer and the rest of the band. It certainly helps explain his sacking in 1962. After all, if you are part of a gang and refuse to go along with gang directives, then soon the gang will rid themselves of you. And that is precisely what happened to Best in 1962.

In fact, out of all The Beatles' relatives it was George's mother who emerges as the most liberal. She told Hunter Davies, 'It's his own hair, I used to say. Why should anyone tell you what to do with what's your own?' Other mothers were not so understanding. After a night at the Cavern, Billy Hatton would take George back to his house for late night refreshments. 'My mum used to look at him,' he recalls, 'because his hair was fairly long – not as long as it became – and I knew what she was thinking, which was, I'll be counting the spoons when he's gone.'

The second faction to use long hair as a means of protest was Britain's small number of Beatniks, many of whom attended art colleges, like John. Although the Beatnik culture, as expressed through its music, was not to his liking – 'We were always anti-jazz, I think it is shit music ... followed by students in Marks and Spencers pullovers', he once sneered – consciously or not, he would have recognised kindred rebel spirits from their hairstyles.

But it was Hamburg, not Liverpool, that sowed the seed for the creation of the famous Beatle haircut.

PRESS CONFERENCE, LOS ANGELES, 1964

JOURNALIST *Have you ever measured your hair to see whose is the longest?*

BEATLES *No.*

The Beatles first saw the cut that would bring them such notoriety when Jürgen Vollmer – and later Astrid Kirchherr and Klaus Voormann – came into the Kaiserkeller club. Because of his hairstyle, Jürgen was very wary of the place he was walking into: 'I knew only too well that an "artsy" type like me with hair combed forward was totally out of place in this rock club, and not at all welcome.'

Once contact had been established with the 'Exis' (as John called them), The Beatles became fascinated by their haircuts. 'Exi' hair was swept not backwards but forwards – and then sideways. Astrid later revealed that the source of this cut was a character in the 1950 Jean Cocteau film *Orpheus*, and that many German boys were wearing it at her college.

During their second Hamburg visit, in March 1961, the Beatles moved into the Top Ten club. One night Jürgen asked if he could film the band at a gig. This proved impossible, so George suggested he shoot a daytime photo session at the club.

As Jürgen recalls, 'During that photo session at the Top Ten, George had combed his hair forward. He kept it that way for the evening in front of the audience. But the next day it was back to its familiar pompadour – "the rockers had given him funny looks", he said.'

It was the adventurous Stuart Sutcliffe who was the next Beatle to try out the 'Exi' style. 'He was the first one who really got the nerve to get the Brylcreem out of his hair,' Astrid recalled in 1995, 'and ask me to cut his hair for him.'

Just as John and Paul liked their girlfriends to dress like Brigitte Bardot, so Astrid liked her boyfriends to wear their hair long. For that reason she often cut Klaus's hair. When she and Stu started seeing each other, it wasn't long before her scissors were back at work.

'Stuart wanted to have the same haircut that Klaus and Jürgen had, so I cut Stuart's hair that way', she explained. 'Then George came along and asked me to cut his hair that way. But Paul and John couldn't decide whether to have the different haircut. It took them quite a long time. I think at least six months or more. They went to Paris to visit Jürgen, who was working there, and they asked him if he would cut their hair for them like his. So I only cut Stuart and George's hair.'

George Harrison also remembered: 'Astrid and Klaus were very influential.

ABOVE Hard to believe that the band's haircuts were considered extreme at the time, but their length became a national talking point and in doing so created the group's nickname, the 'Mop Tops'. Here the band pose in Sweden in 1963.

I remember we went to the swimming baths and my hair was down from the water and they said, "No, leave it, it's good." I didn't have my Vaseline anyway and I was thinking, well, these people are cool – if they think it is good, I'll leave it like this. They gave me that confidence and when it dried off it dried naturally down, which later became "The Look". Before that, as a rocker, I wore my hair back, although it would never go back without a fight.'

It would be during John and Paul's Paris holiday in 1961 that their Teddy Boy style would be altered for ever. After hooking up with Jürgen – and realising that their rocker look would get them nowhere with the young ladies of Paris – John and Paul not only bought new clothes but also asked Jürgen to cut their hair in his hotel room.

'He had his hair Mod style', McCartney remembered. 'We said, "Would you do our hair like yours?" We're on holiday – what the hell. We're buying capes and pantaloons, throwing caution to the wind. He said, "No, boys, I like you as rockers, you look great." But we begged him enough, so he said all right. He didn't do it quite the same as his. His was actually more coming over to one side. A kind of long-haired Hitler thing, and we'd wanted that, so it was really a bit of an accident. We sat down in his hotel and he just got it – the "Beatle" cut.

'When we got back to Liverpool it was all, "Eh, your hair's has gone funny." – "No, this is the new style." We nearly tried to change it back but it wouldn't go, it kept flapping forward. And that just caught on ... It was great for us because we never had to style it or anything. – Wash it, towel it, turn upside down and give it a shake, and that was it. Everyone thought we had started it, so it became the Beatle hairdo.'

Billy Shepherd's book *The True Story of The Beatles* recalls how John nearly reverted to type: '"It's getting a bit too long now", said John, a week after they returned to Liverpool. "I'll comb it back again." He brushed like mad but nothing happened. "I think it wants to stay like that", commented Paul, who was happy to keep his fringe. So John and Paul kept their Hamburg/Paris styles.'

In a tough town like Liverpool, looking different took real courage. 'The boys were an easy target for troublemakers who attended those early dates', Neil Aspinall confirmed to the authoritative fanzine *Beatlefan*. 'Gangs would often make a point of shouting insults at them. It was their childish way of looking for a fight or getting back at the Beatles because their girls thought so much of the group. ... At Latham Hall, which is in the Seaforth suburb of Liverpool, two troublemakers followed Stu into the dressing room muttering things like "Get your hair cut, girl." John and Pete saw this and went after them. A fight broke out and John broke his little finger. To this day the smallest finger of his right hand is slightly bent. It set crooked and never straightened.'

It was worth the hassle. The hairstyle gave the band an absolutely unique look not only in Liverpool but throughout the country. And that was worth every skirmish.

Beatles Monthly: 'They realised the tremendous advantages of the instant recognition of their hairstyle and went to great lengths before every appearance, to make sure everything was as it should be. John particularly, as always, moaning about the fact that his hair would not go into place. He found it very difficult to keep the Beatle haircut looking as it should. Paul was also very strong on looking exactly right and got most annoyed if his forehead showed at any time.'

It is instructive to study a photograph taken around this time of Paul McCartney and Ivor Jay of The Jaywalkers at a sparsely attended Beatles gig in Aldershot. There Macca sits, slightly imperious in his black leather jacket and early Beatle haircut, and there stands the Jaywalker, dressed in a dowdy suit, with different-coloured waistcoat, tie, hanky in top pocket, looking like a prosperous newsagent. And good for him. But one is the past, the other the future.

When the band decided to let Pete Best go and hired Ringo, one of the first rules of his joining concerned his hair. 'You can keep the sidies [sideburns],' Lennon told him over the phone, 'but lose the beard.'

Ringo confirms: 'They all changed my image. I used to have my hair right back like a Teddy Boy with a Tony Curtis cut and sideboards, and suddenly it was "shave them off and put your hair down", which I did.'

OPPOSITE The band at the start of the 'Mop Top' look. The style was first seen by the band in Hamburg, and John and Paul had their hair cut in this style by Jürgen Vollmer in Paris in 1961.

PRESS CONFERENCE, LOS ANGELES, 1964

REPORTER *What excuse do you have for your collar length hair?*
RINGO *Well, it grows out of my head.*
JOHN *We don't need an excuse. You need an excuse.*
REPORTER *Do you ever get dandruff with all that hair?*
JOHN *We have dandruff occasionally, you know, just like normal people.*
REPORTER *Do you have any plans for a haircut?*
GEORGE *We don't make plans like that, our manager does …*

When it all took off for them – when success was literally here, there and everywhere – their haircuts caused a sensation. Manufacturers now started producing Beatle wigs. By the thousand. There was a Beatle hairspray, Beatle combs, Beatle hairbrushes.

Hairdressers acted quickly. A firm called Andre Bernard of Mayfair (ironically, McCartney's brother Michael worked in their Liverpool shop), for example, began advertising Beatle haircuts. 'Brush hair into nape of neck at back and from crown at front', they advised; 'brush hair down into heavy fringe, and bring small section of hair at each side in front of ear.'

Granada TV even brought the band in on 27 November 1963 to appear with Ken Dodd on their show *Late Scene Extra* just to talk about hair. Interviewed by a young Gay Byrne, Ken Dodd took over the proceedings with surreal and funny one-liners, and the subject was left unexplored.

Rave magazine reported: 'In the unlikely event of your not having a Beatle haircut – get one! It need not tie you down to being John, Paul or any one of those because practically everybody but Frank Sinatra has one now.' They certainly did, and Lennon quickly got annoyed at his contemporaries for following the leaders.

'Why can't these copyists make their own style like we did', he complained. 'It happens in hairstyles as well. I see players in some groups have even the same length of hair as us. It's no good them saying they are students and they just happen to have long hair. We were students as well, before we came to London and we didn't have this hairstyle then, did we?'

The fuss made about the band's hair crossed the Atlantic. When The Beatles' American record company, Capitol Records, sat down to decide how to promote the band, hair was the element they decided to use as they went on the attack.

In the 28 December 1963 edition of *Billboard*, adverts appeared showing four similar-looking haircuts with the slogan 'The Beatles Are Coming!', thus ensuring that two months before they reached America their hair – not their music – was the major topic of conversation.

On 1 January 1964 Capitol Records issued a memo to their sales people. Sent by Paul Russell, the company's National Album Merchandising Manager, to sales and regional managers, it read: 'Shortly after the 1st you'll have bulk quantities of a Beatle hairdo wig. As soon as they arrive – and until further notice – you and each of your sales promotion staff are to wear the wig during the business day. Next, see how many of the retail clerks in your area have a sense of humor. Then, try your jocks, especially those who hold teen dance hops. Then, offer some to jocks and stores for promotions. Get these Beatle wigs around properly, and you'll find you're helping to start the Beatle Hair Do Craze that should be sweeping the country soon.'

On his first night in New York, Ringo did a transatlantic interview with the DJ Brian Matthew. Naturally, the subject of hair was brought up.

'You proved that you don't wear wigs, I hope', Matthew asked.

'Yeah', Ringo replied.

'What did you do?'

'Took them off.'

An American fan writing in *Beatlefan* said of that time: 'But there was no way we were going to miss The Beatles, even if we had never even heard of them till a few days before. If nothing else, we just had to see if their hair was really as long as we'd heard.'

After their appearance on the *Ed Sullivan Show*, watched by a record-breaking audience of 70 million, Americans fell in love with The Beatles. But the newspapers did not, and they used their hair to get at the band.

'Seventy-five per cent publicity, 20 per cent hair cut and five per cent lilting lament', said the *New York Herald Tribune*. 'The only thing that is different is the hair as far as I can see. I give them a year', said another writer.

Time magazine would later talk about The Beatles' 'mushroom haircuts', while *Newsweek* reported that 'When Dick Clark played "She Loves You" on his TV show, the disc averaged a mediocre 73 score. According to Clark, when the kids saw a photo of four long-haired lads, they just laughed.'

The fact was, many American males viewed Beatle hair as highly effeminate. If Britain swore by the short-back-and-sides cut, then America pledged allegiance to the crew cut. The crew cut was short and severe. It derived from the US Army and thus spoke of courage and a strong patriotism.

Beatle hair was a direct attack on those values. Christopher Makris recalls: 'It was common to be sent home from school if you weren't wearing appropriate dress or if your hair was too long. Another friend, who went to a private Catholic school, was marched along with four other boys to the local barber for having hair that went an inch or so past the collar. The story made the *New York Times*, believe it or not.'

Hair could also bring out the worst in people. At a reception in Washington after The Beatles' début American concert, a female guest approached Ringo from the back and actually cut off a lock of his hair. From then on, such high-class parties would swiftly be avoided by the band.

Not long afterwards, early Beatles' photographer Dezo Hoffmann walked out on the band because of their hair and their egos.

'During the Beatles' visit to Miami, John Lennon gave me very good reason not to follow them any longer', he revealed. 'It was quite a silly argument. I took a picture of him being taught how to water-ski. He had no hair on his forehead (because it was blown back). John was terribly vain. That was his only fault. I was annoyed that he yelled at me in front of everyone. He treated me like a five-year-old so I just turned my back and left. I never saw them again.'

REPORTER *Those are funny haircuts aren't they?*
JOHN *We don't think they're funny, you see.*
REPORTER *Who chooses your clothes?*
JOHN *We choose our own. Who chose yours?*
REPORTER *My husband. Now tell me, are there any subjects you would prefer not to discuss?*
JOHN *Yes. Your husband.*

In 1965 the band released the *Rubber Soul* album. The album cover was a head-and-shoulders shot of the band, with their hair longer and thicker than it had ever been. In fact, the eye-catching quality of this photograph is the luxuriant hair itself, beautifully framing those famous faces and undoubtedly aggravating every strait-laced adult who happened to gaze upon this sleeve.

As for getting their own haircuts, the band tended to use hairdressers they met on TV or films sets, exclusive outlets – George often went to Leonard's in London's exclusive Mayfair district – or their wives. Maureen Starr, Ringo's wife, was a qualified hairdresser and always cut his hair for him. In return, he often spoke about buying his wife a chain of hairdressing salons.

Ringo had a thing about hairdressers. In his early days as a Beatle, when they were constantly being asked how long their fame would last, he once said, 'I could see myself packing up drumming, putting on a black coat and striped trousers and wandering through the salons asking "Is everything all right, madam?" or "Would you perhaps care for a cup of tea?" I'm still interested in this as a possible career. After all, girls always want to have their hair styled, don't they?'

When Mike Maxfield of The Dakotas bought his wife a hair salon, Ringo publicly expressed his disappointment to *Fab 208* that he had not acted quicker. In fact, he never did acquire any premises for Maureen.

Later on, while the band was touring Australia, two fans in Melbourne got to use scissors on the boys' hair. George had left for a scenic mountain drive, but John, Paul and Ringo accepted an offer from two fans, Val Behrens and Grace Ferringo, to cut their hair prior to a gig. Afterwards – one assumes with the band's blessing – the girls stood outside the Festival Hall and tried to sell some of the locks of the band's hair, but no one believed they were genuine.

In 1966 the band asked their old friend Klaus Voormann to design the cover for their sixth studio album, *Revolver*. The resulting and striking graphic he produced

ABOVE AND RIGHT Ringo and John with the 'Mop Top' look, while Mr Noel Gallagher, of Oasis, sports a Beatle-type hairstyle.

OPPOSITE And it shall be written and decreed that no Beatle forehead will ever be seen in public. Paul, John and George in Southend in 1963.

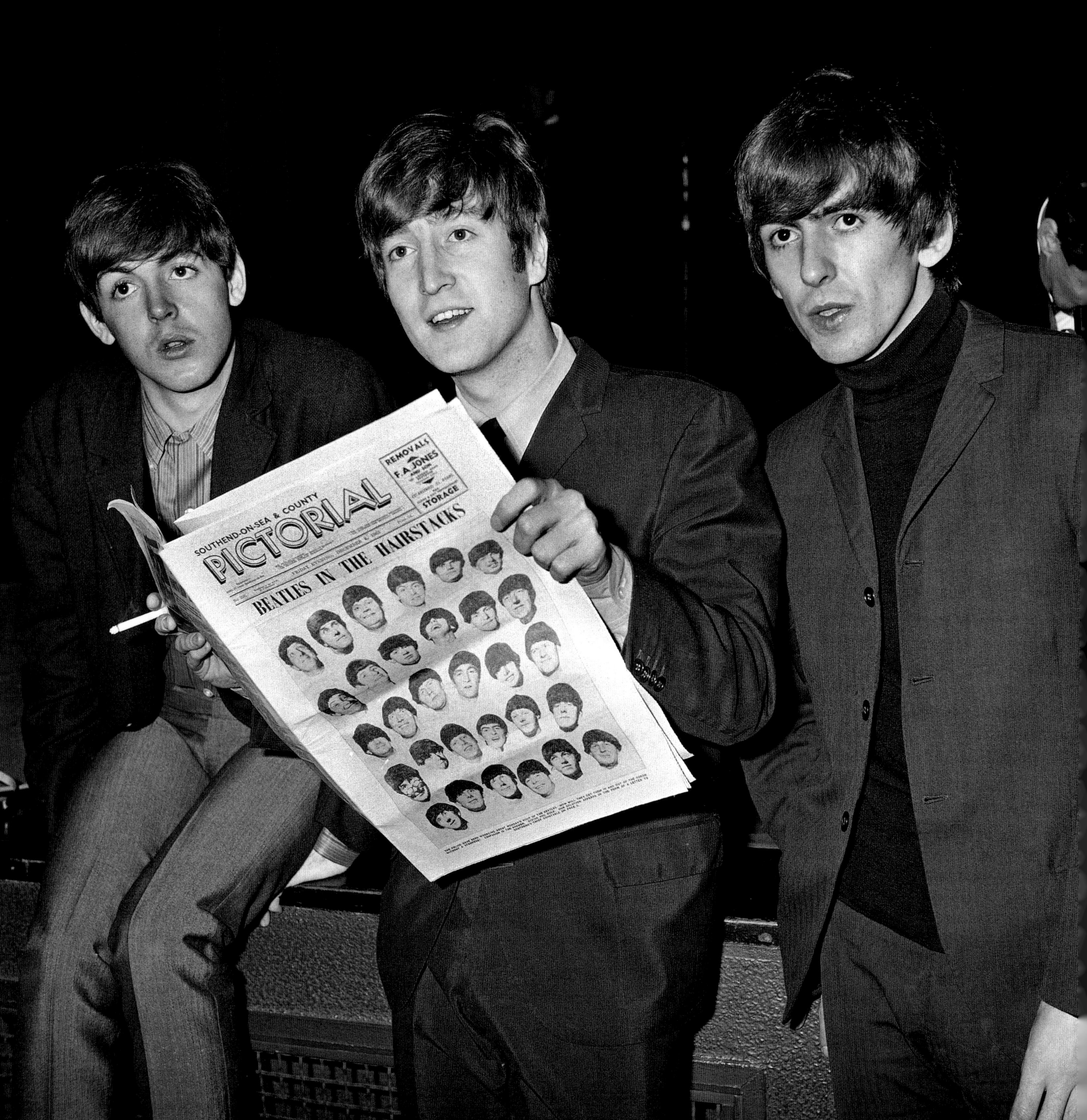
SOUTHEND-ON-SEA & COUNTY
PICTORIAL
REMOVALS
F.A. JONES
STORAGE
BEATLES IN THE HAIRSTACKS

was inspired by the band's hair and the public fuss over the subject, he later revealed. Voormann's drawing depicted the four Beatles with various images placed in and around their hair. In August of the same year that that landmark album was released, The Beatles toured America. On the 20th they held a press conference to which only Beatle fans aged under eighteen were invited. One of the questions directed at John was, 'When did you last go to the barber's?' He replied, 'I haven't been to a barber's for years. George often cuts my hair when we are on the road and Cyn does it when I am at home.'

Beatle hair was a valuable asset, a fact recognised by John when he had his hair cut by Klaus Baruch at 7.30 in the morning of Tuesday 6 September 1966 for his appearance as a soldier in the Dick Lester film *How I Won The War*. Baruch shaved off Lennon's sideburns, cut back the sides and then swept the fringe back and greased it down. Lennon's cut hair was then ceremonially burnt so as to stop anyone selling it. That's how important and popular this band were.

PRESS CONFERENCE, NEW YORK, 1964

REPORTER *Where do your hair-dos originate from?*

GEORGE *Our scalps.*

The man who would be the most heavily associated with Beatle hair was fifteen years old when he went to meet his mother at a hairdresser's in north London. The young Leslie Cavendish walked in, saw the shop owner surrounded by a bevy of pretty girls and thought, 'This is the job I want to do.' He got himself an apprenticeship at Vidal Sassoon, first in Bond Street and then later at the Grosvenor House Hotel (where a young Michael Barrymore also worked).

Among Leslie's regular customers was Jane Asher, at that time Paul McCartney's girlfriend. 'Of course,' says Leslie, 'we all knew who her boyfriend was, but of course it would be far too uncool to ever mention him.'

It was Jane who brought his name up. Would Leslie consider coming over to St John's Wood and cutting her boyfriend's hair later that day? Paul had been busy working and needed a trim. Leslie acted all nonchalant. He was a keen football man (he had considered soccer as a profession once), and his team, QPR, had a big game that day, which he didn't want to miss.

On the other hand, he didn't want to miss the chance to cut one of the most famous heads of hair in the world. 'Would six be OK?', he asked tentatively. 'Perfect', replied Jane.

Intrigued by the fact that Paul McCartney lived on a street that shared his surname (Cavendish Avenue), Leslie showed up, as promised, at about six that evening.

It wasn't hard to figure out which house he was expected at. The gaggle of fans standing outside number 7 told him exactly where he needed to be. Cavendish rang the buzzer by the gate. The next thing he knew, Paul McCartney was striding down his driveway to meet him. The smiling Beatle opened the gate, greeted the fans, posed for photographs, gave autographs and then said to Leslie, 'Come on in and do my barnet.' ('Barnet' is Cockney rhyming slang: 'Barnet Fair' = hair.)

'I remember as we walked to the door,' Cavendish recalls, 'he had his Aston Martin to his left, and there was only one other person in my mind who had such a car – and that was James Bond.'

After introductions and pleasantries they went upstairs to Macca's bathroom, where Leslie washed and shaped the hair, nervous as hell that he was treating an original 'Mop Top'.

'It still wasn't long, and it still wasn't literally on the forehead but the shape was still there', he recalls.

After the cut, McCartney took the hairdresser downstairs, where he played him rough demos for the *Sgt Pepper* album. All the time McCartney was nothing but good-natured. Moreover, he liked Cavendish's work, especially his ability to make his hair look long when in fact it was quite short. Cavendish achieved this illusion by layering the hair using his fingers rather than a comb. The technique (learned at Vidal Sassoon's) kept McCartney's hair smart but also aligned it with the current fashion towards much longer hair.

Within a few months Leslie Cavendish was one of the most famous hairdressers in the land.

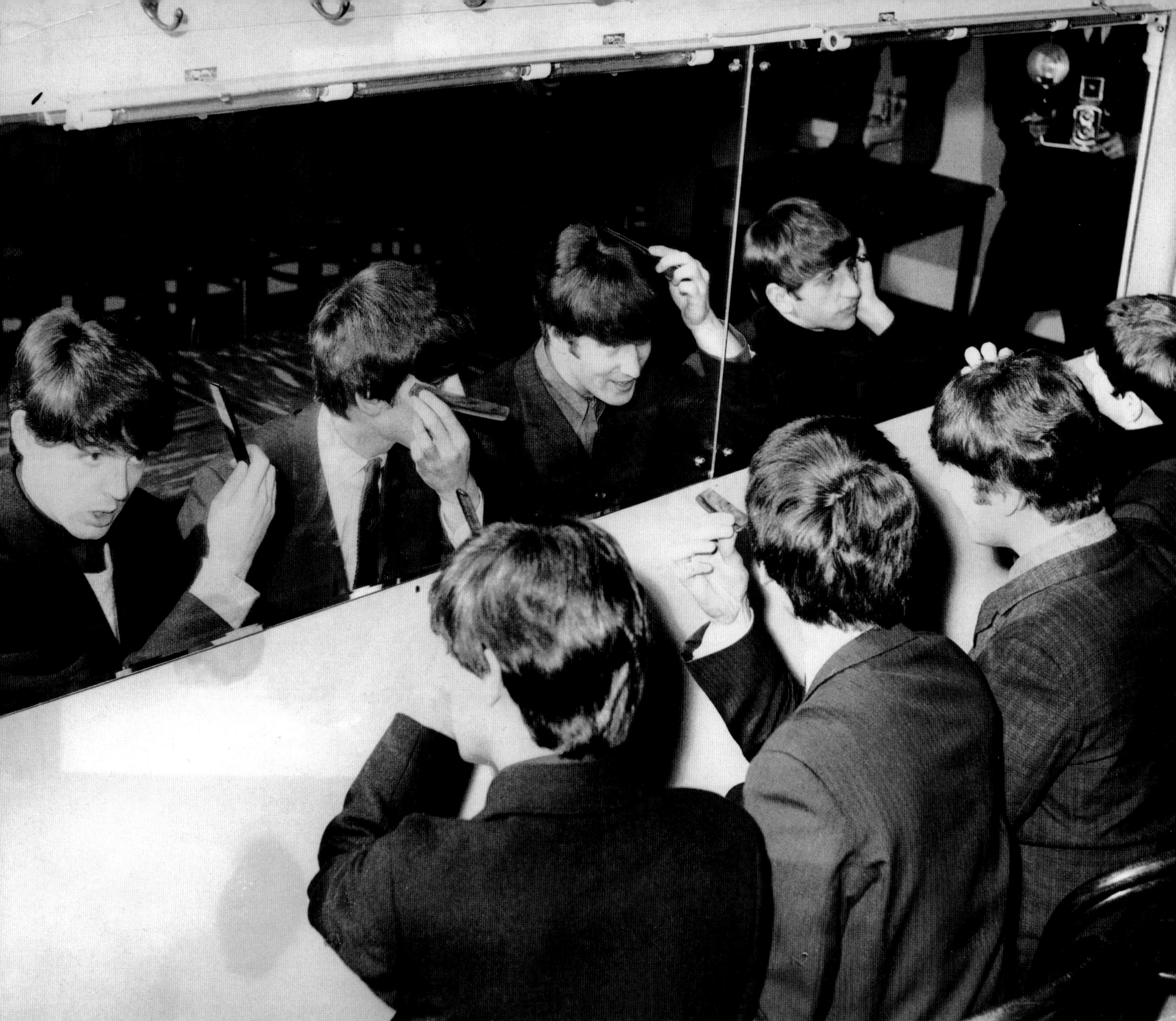

ABOVE Forward-combing in Leicester in 1964.

THE BEATLES

OPPOSITE AND ABOVE The Beatles arrive in America, where their hair quickly became a huge talking point. At almost every press conference they attended around the world the band would routinely be asked about the length of their hair.

FOLLOWING PAGES Two album covers that relate to the band's hair. The cover of *Rubber Soul* (1965) deliberately highlighted the length and thickness of the band's hair. And Klaus Voormann, who designed the sleeve for *Revolver* (1966), later said that his first point of inspiration for his drawing was their hair, as this was one of the first things people thought about when they heard the word 'Beatles'.

NEW IMPROVED FULL DIMENSIONAL STEREO
RUBBER SOUL
Capitol

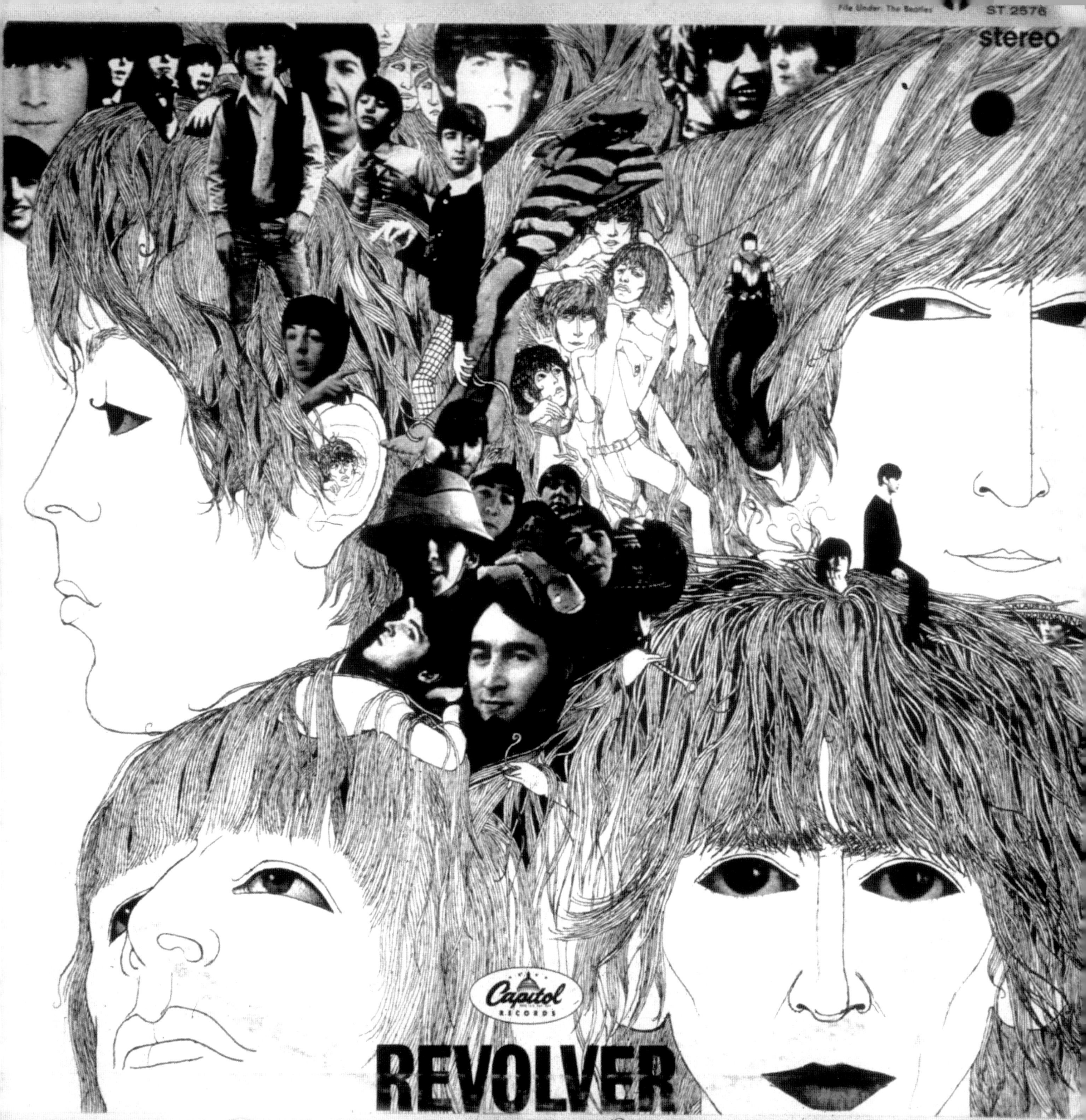
File Under: The Beatles
ST 2576
stereo
Capitol
RECORDS
REVOLVER

ABOVE, OPPOSITE AND FOLLOWING PAGES The Beatles fully supported the Hippies' 'Love and Peace' movement, and it was George who first grew his hair long as a signal of approval. Brian Epstein would not have been happy, given the distaste the country at large felt for 'long-haired layabouts'. Meanwhile, John and Paul were content to have their hair styled by the hip hairdresser Leslie Cavendish, and Ringo looked to his wife, Maureen, a professional hairdresser, to keep his hair in shape.

ABOVE AND RIGHT Three Beatles with a cut-out of John from the *Yellow Submarine* film. John had now started growing his hair. Later on he would refuse to cut his hair until wars in the world had ceased. Unfortunately for mankind, his hair grew very, very long ...

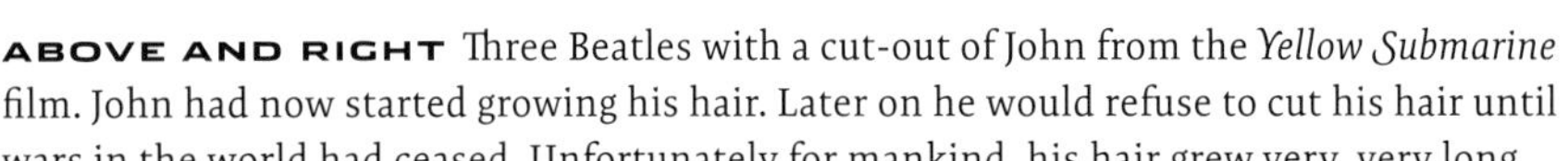

OPPOSITE Through layering and other techniques Leslie Cavendish was able to sustain the illusion that McCartney had very long hair. Yet, as this photo shows, it was no thicker or longer than previous incarnations.

ABOVE AND OPPOSITE With Yoko by his side John would now start radically transforming himself. The beard and the long hair would have been unimaginable a year previously, in 1968, but with his interest in being a Beatle waning considerably, John now wanted to express himself in different ways. George felt the same way, and their hair and beards started to mirror their lack of interest in maintaining Beatleworld.

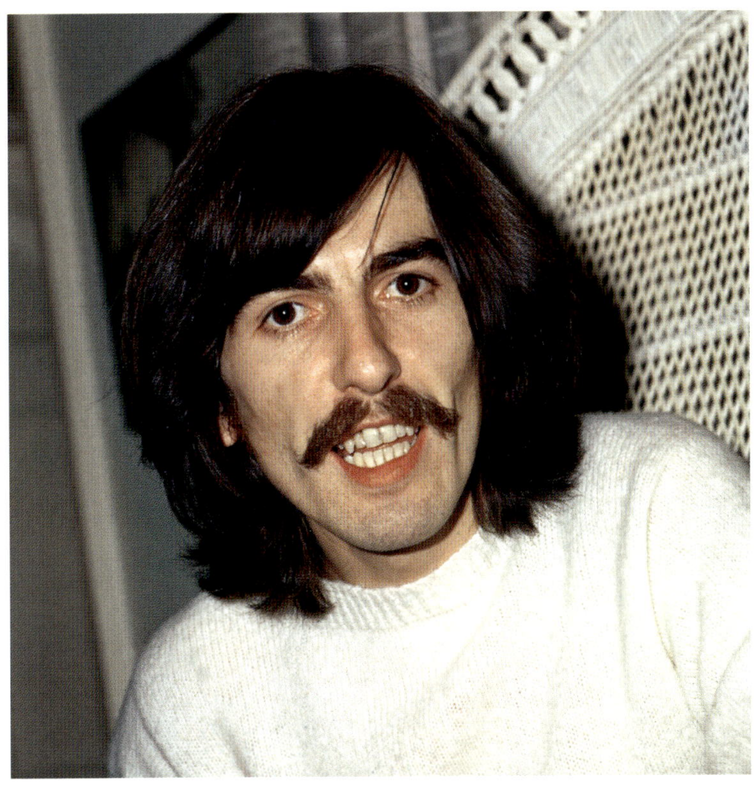

OPPOSITE AND ABOVE RIGHT AND FOLLOWING PAGE · LEFT Ringo grew his hair a little but, unlike the others, kept to his Dandy style.

FOLLOWING PAGE · RIGHT John and Yoko in their famous bed in for peace at the Amsterdam Hilton hotel in March 1969. Contrast John with a 1962 photo, and you can see how far, stylistically, this man and his band have travelled.

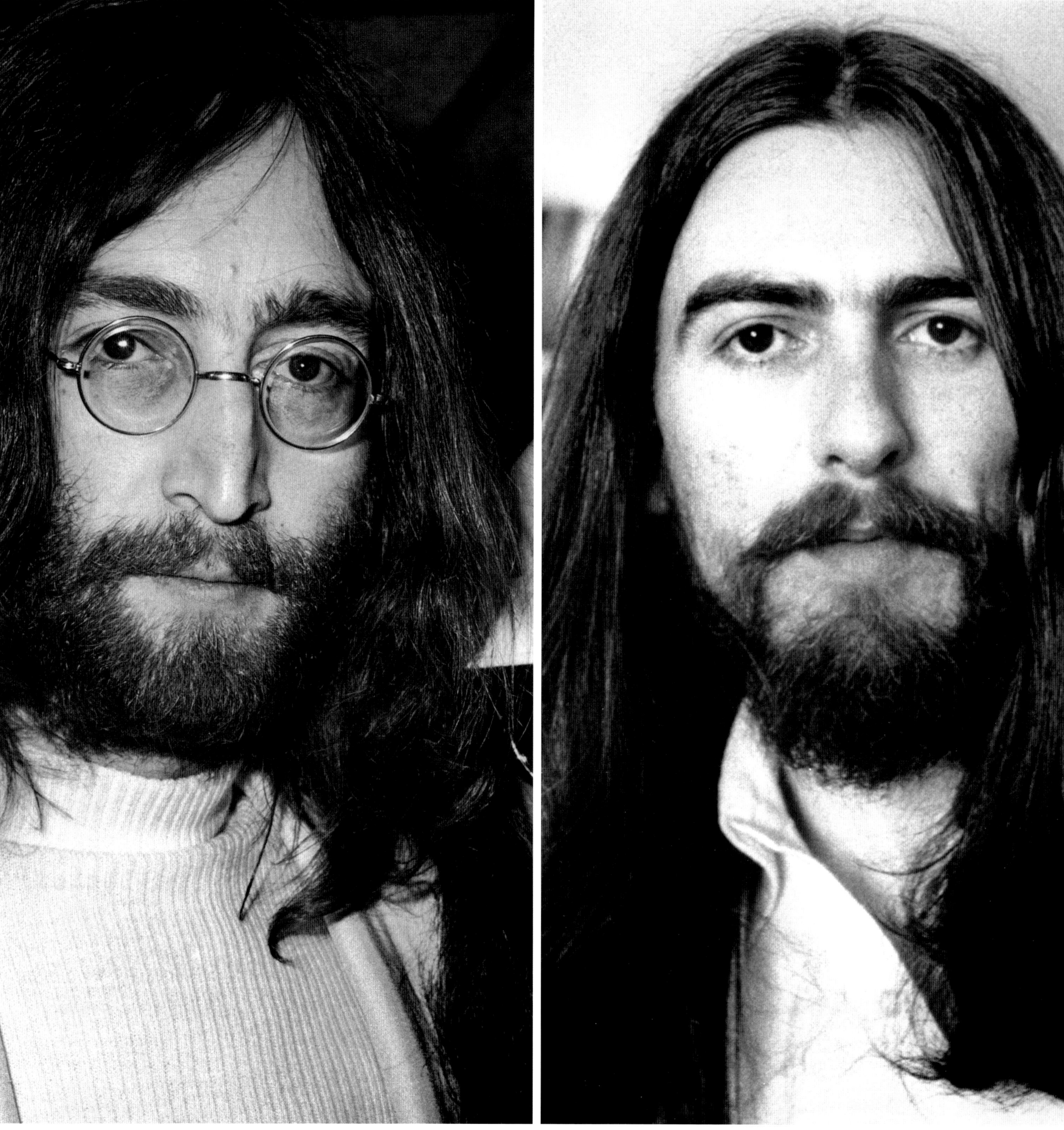

OPPOSITE AND ABOVE In 1969 John and George were Paul's biggest obstacles as they wrangled over the future of the band, which is why the two men started looking very much alike.

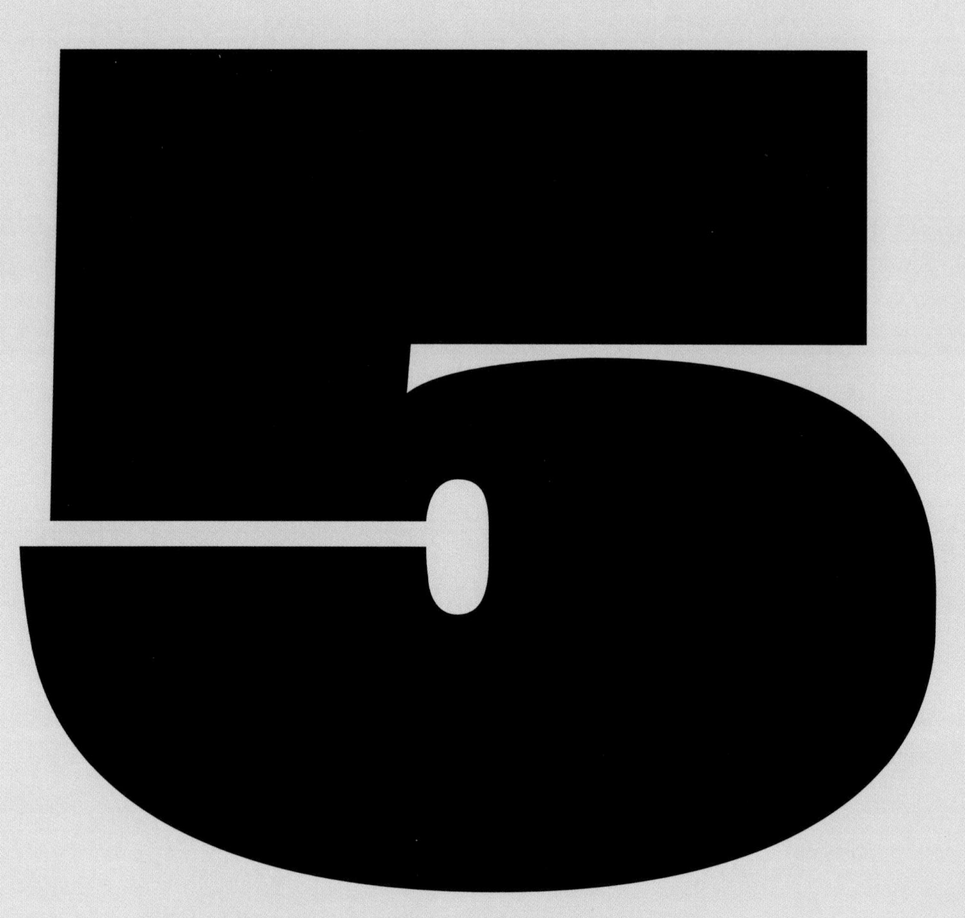

BANK

THE LITTLE SHOP ON THE CORNER

Chapter Five

'We should never have tried to beat Marks and Spencers with the boutique idea.'

PAUL McCARTNEY

In February 1964 *Rave* magazine was launched. Aimed at a young male audience fixated on pop and fashion, the first edition carried an interview with John Lennon. When asked about his future, he stated: 'That's another dream of mine. To own some clothing stores. Just providing the best gear. ... I'd probably buy most of it myself ... that's where most of my money goes nowadays.'

In 1967 he got his wish. Early on in that remarkable year of their career, The Beatles were told by their accountants, Bryce Hanmer, that they could either pay the government £2 million in taxes or spend it themselves. What was it going to be? Their answer was Apple, a multimedia company that they would oversee.

There would be Apple Records, Apple Books, Apple Films, Apple Clothes, Apple everything – that was the vision, a chance to use their huge fortune to unearth talent in various fields and allow people to shine. With their money they would create a hip capitalism that would benefit all. It was an idea much in keeping with the anti-capitalist ideas that they were being exposed to by the counterculture movement.

'The aim of the company', Lennon said, 'isn't a stack of gold teeth in the bank. We've done that bit already.'

'We've already bought our dreams', McCartney announced. 'We want to share that possibility with others.'

One of their first ideas was to open a clothes shop, a place where people could access the kind of clothing the band were picking up in the King's Road, but at much more affordable prices. 'What a great idea,' Mark Lewisohn tells me, 'this idea that anybody could now pick up groovy clothing at a good price.'

It would cost a lot to achieve, but then neither Lennon nor Harrison was averse to sharing some of their wealth with friends. At the end of 1964 they had both put money into buying a supermarket on Hayling Island, which they then handed to their friend Pete Shotton to run as general manager.

OPPOSITE John and Paul return from New York, having launched Apple in the USA. Paul is following John's penchant for the colour white and thus making their clothes present a united front, when in reality Beatleworld was starting to fall apart.

Over the next two years Shotton made a success of the business, which encouraged Lennon to ask him to move to London and run the proposed Apple shop. Shotton recalls Lennon declaring, 'We could sell 'em anything. If The Beatles started wearing a jacket with one arm torn off, the whole world would want to wear it. We could make a fucking fortune.'

The location of the shop was easy to decide. In early 1967 The Beatles had purchased a three-floor building at 94 Baker Street. It was agreed that the Apple organisation would be run from the top floor of this building, and the other two floors would be put aside for the Apple shop. (Apple would later move to Wigmore Street and then Savile Row.) McCartney's idea was that everything in the store would be for sale, including the furniture, the display cases and the light fittings. There would be clothes, of course, but also jewellery, paintings, posters, records – anything that caught the imagination.

Having been impressed by The Fool's clothes for the 'All You Need Is Love' session (although Ringo did moan about his outfit weighing him down as he played the drums), the band asked if the company would now come up with several designs for clothes that would be in keeping with the prevailing psychedelic fashion.

'We started an Apple clothes shop because we were dressing in such interesting clothes and The Fool were making a lot of them', McCartney remembered. 'So we said, could you make a few pieces that we could take to other people and they could manufacture stuff to your designs?'

Shotton agreed to Lennon's proposition but told the band it would be some time before the shop would be ready. The Beatles disagreed; they wanted the shop opened within five weeks.

Shotton quickly started the shop's renovation, and his memories of this time reveal much about the rift developing between John and Paul. Shotton later recalled how McCartney would arrive at the shop and give a specific design instruction. He would then leave. Lennon would then arrive and give a completely different direction. McCartney would then come back and ask if his initial instruction had been followed ... And so it went.

Shotton also harboured a lot of reservations about The Fool.

'Simon, Marijke and Josje looked as if they had stepped right out of the pages of a Grimm's fairy tale or J.R.R. Tolkien's *Lord of the Rings*', he wrote. 'They invariably wore hand-woven costumes of brilliantly coloured silks, satins and velvets, said to represent such elements as Fire, Water or Air.'

His first run-in occurred quite early on in his relationship with the company. The Fool had asked that all the labels in their clothes be hand-stitched and made out of silk. Shotton looked at the figures and realised that the labels would now cost even more than the clothes themselves. He went to Lennon with his calculations, but the Beatle ignored his concerns. 'Remember, Pete, we're not business freaks, we're artists – that's what Apple is all about – artists', Lennon told his close ally. Case dismissed.

The Fool's next move was to take a ten-day trip to Morocco to buy fabrics and jewellery. Morocco was the 'in' place for the hip London scene, and the band footed the bill.

They then started presenting numerous designs. There was an orange embossed velvet coat with long sleeves, brocaded trouser suits, outdoor coats with heavy tapestry, mini-skirts with long dresses which could be added for evening wear. There were a huge number of tops, either for girls or boys. They all had names such as Sunflower, Peter Pan, Daisy, Violet, Cosmic, Bluebell, Honeybee (designed for adults and children), Mustapha's Dream, Mercury, Milky Way, Astral Planet, The Nazz, Valentine and Polaris.

Typically each item broke itself down as follows: the cloth would cost about 15 shillings, the lining 7 to 8 shillings, the zip between 2 and 3 shillings, and the cost of a worker putting the outfit together about 30 shillings. For Apple to make a profit on these items, the shop would have to charge somewhere in the region of £15. The average weekly wage in 1968 was £10.

Marijke and Josje's designs, The Fool announced to the world, sought to combine elements from many different cultures. Fool member Simon Posthuma stated, 'All the people of the earth are forced to come together now and this expresses itself even in fashion.'

Barry Miles in his biography *Paul McCartney: Many Years From Now* is a little less grandiose. He claims the clothes 'looked more like fancy dress costumes than anything one could wear day-to-day: court jester crossed with harlequin crossed with Peter Pan, rainbow colours, zigzag hems, Kate Greenaway layers of flowing fabrics, ballet tights and operatic coats for flower children.'

It was a complaint echoed throughout the Apple empire: the clothes were impractical in both design and style. As Ben Stagg, who worked for Mayfair PR – the company that looked after Brian Epstein's 'Sunday at the Saville' shows (which included such acts as the Four Tops and Jimi Hendrix and soon became must-attend events for London's hip community) – explained: 'All manufacturers work to standard fittings so that when anybody goes into a shop and buys a jumper in small, medium or large, it will fit. The Fool didn't bother with the standard rule of clothes selling, hence you had to be a specific shape to get into one of their costumes.'

The Fool did not just stop at clothes and jewellery. They also had a big part in designing the shop's exterior, as Marijke reveals.

'The Beatles had already acquired the Apple building on Baker Street,' she writes, 'and it was quite boring, so they approached us to have a meeting with all four of them and Brian Epstein during which we came to an agreement to paint the whole building inside and out and mass-produce a clothing and art print line.

'As the lead artist, I designed and made the sketches for the interior and exterior Apple murals and the interior staircase design (something out of the Arabian Nights) first for their approval. The Genie on the exterior was a synthesis of different cultures/religions, influenced by psychedelics. The sketches were done in gouache on paper and the murals in enamel house paint. For the exterior I used the grid technique to transfer the design to the wall; the interior murals were done freehand.

OPPOSITE An original design from The Fool, who submitted nearly a hundred such items for the Apple shop. The inset picture is of the famous Apple label, which cost nearly as much to manufacture as the suit itself.

DESIGNED BY THE FOOL
THIS GARMENT SHOULD BE
DRY CLEANED DRY CLEANED

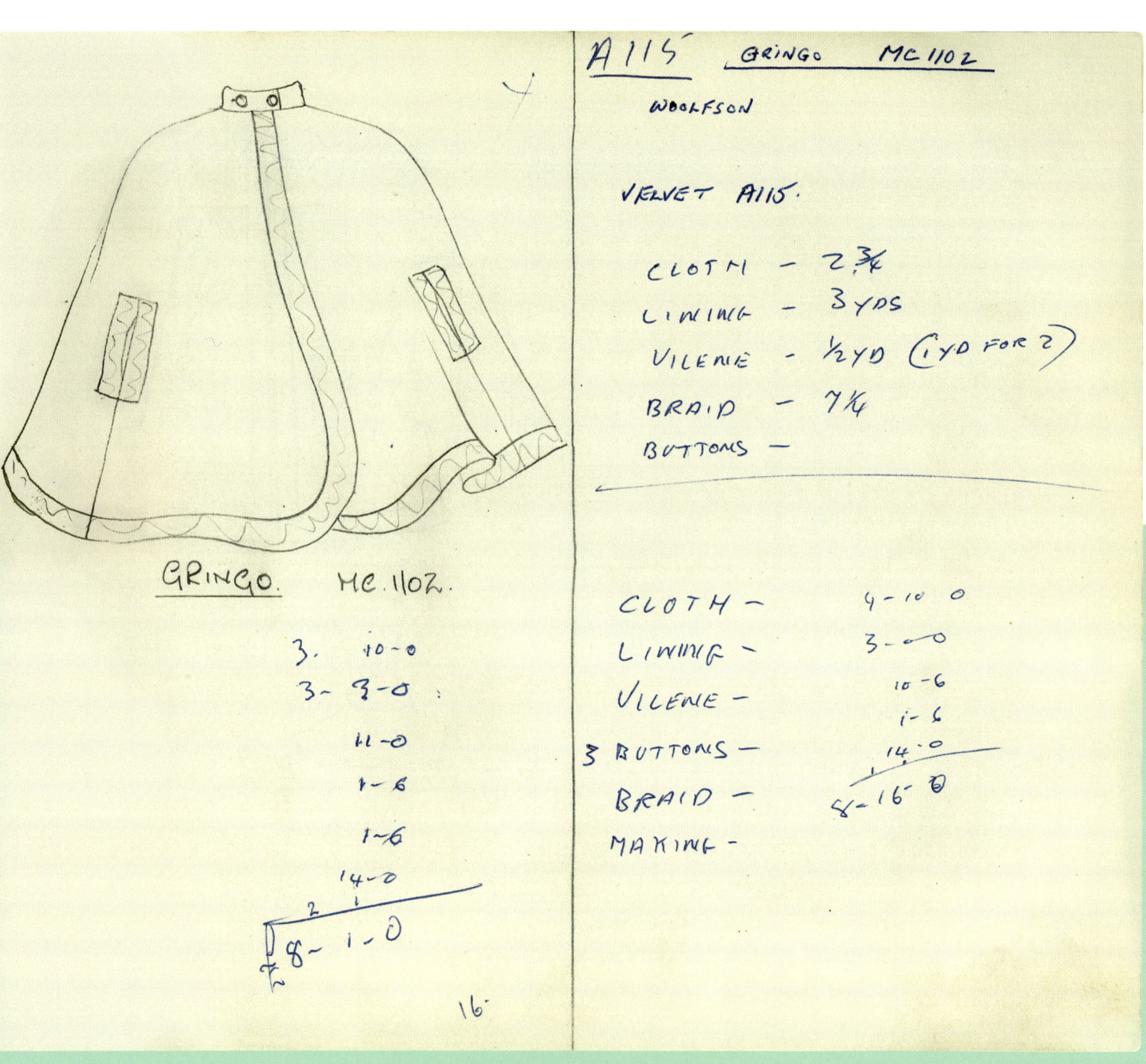
GRINGO. MC.1102.
3. 10-0
3- 8-0
11-0
1-6
1-6
14-0
8- 1-0
16

A115 GRINGO MC1102
WOOLFSON
VELVET A115.
CLOTH - 2¾
LINING - 3 YDS
VILENE - ½ YD (1 YD FOR 2)
BRAID - 7¼
BUTTONS -

CLOTH - 4-10 0
LINING - 3-0-0
VILENE - 10-6
1-6
3 BUTTONS - 14-0
BRAID - 8-16-0
MAKING -

ABOVE, OPPOSITE AND FOLLOWING PAGES Original costing details from John Lyndon's book detailing all the expenses for various Fool clothing items.

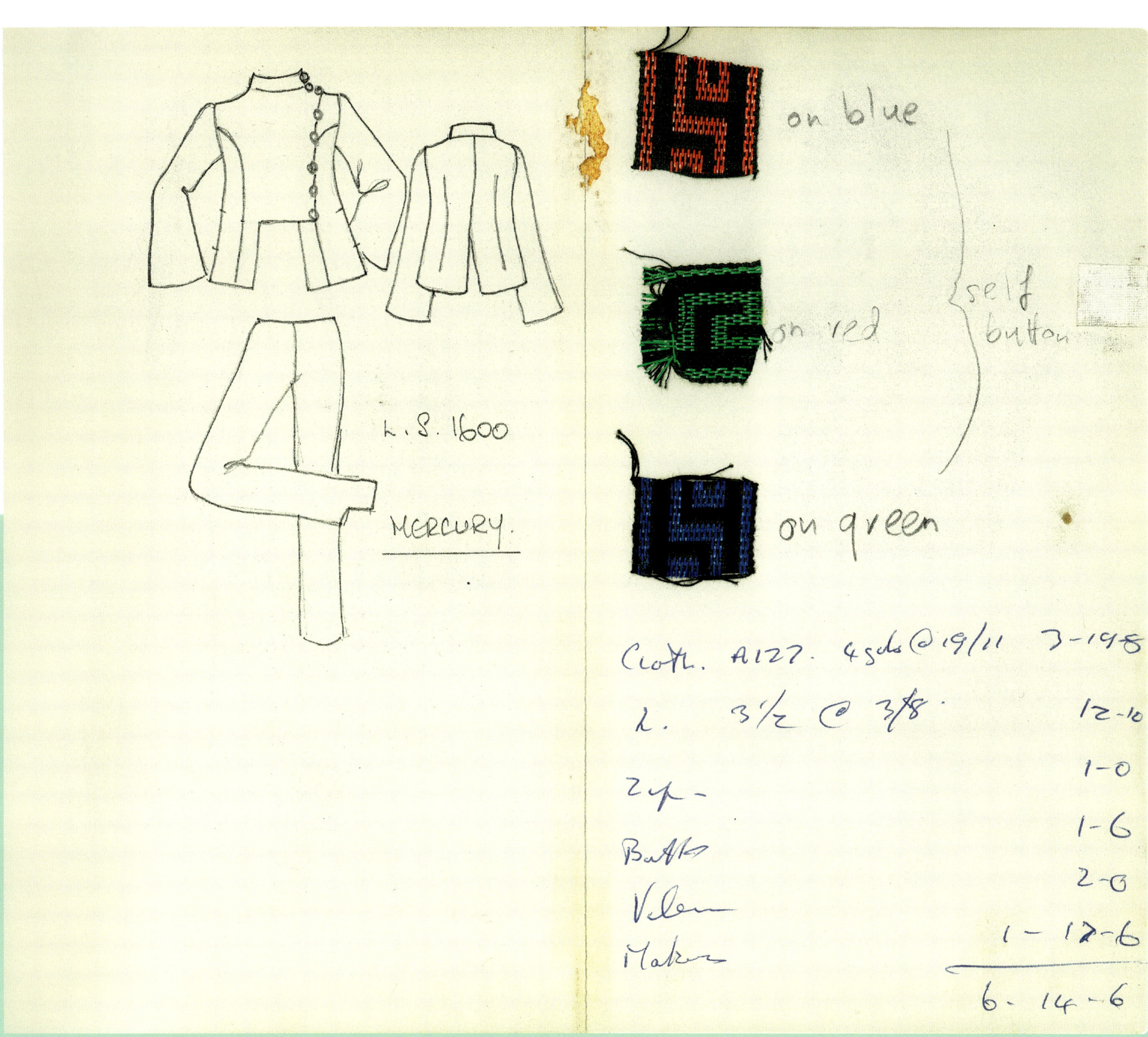

on blue
self button
on red
on green
L. S. 1600
MERCURY.
Cloth. A127. 4 yds @ 19/11 3-19-8
L. 3½ @ 3/8. 12-10
Zip - 1-0
Butts 1-6
Velcro 2-0
Makers 1-17-6
6-14-6

POLARIS. M.B. 1303.

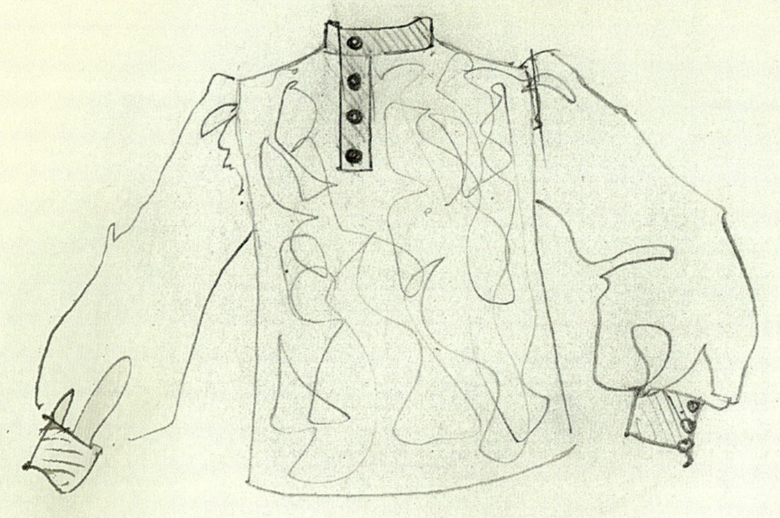

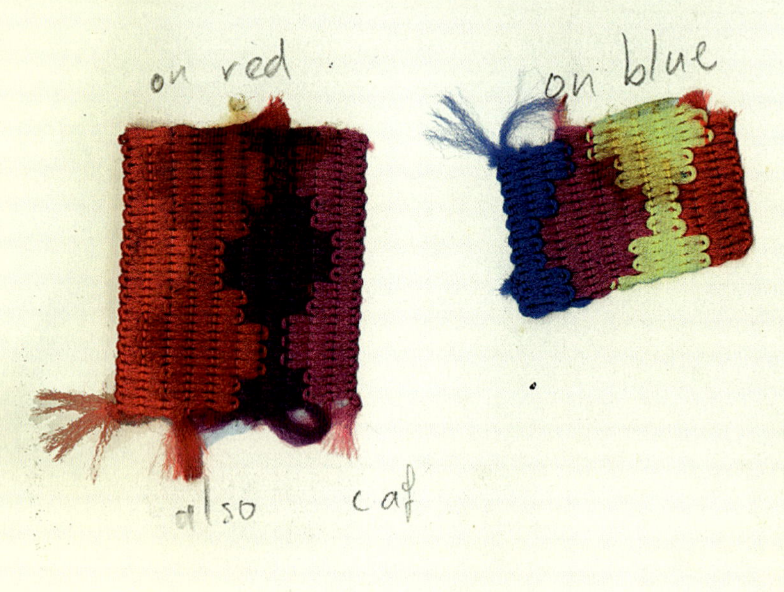

A131

HARRISS

SINGLE COL COMB $1\frac{7}{8}$ yds.

LINING BODY ONLY $1\frac{3}{8}$.

---

2. COL COMB.

BODY 34"

COLLAR/SL/CUFF 1 yd.

LINING. BODY ONLY $1\frac{3}{8}$

VILENE $\frac{3}{8}$ FOR 2.

Braid. $1\frac{1}{2}$ yds @ 4/-

CLOTH @ 18/6.	1-15-6
LINING @ 2/8	4-0
VILENE	6
8 BUTTONS red + blue little buttons	1-4
MAKING	1-5-0
Braid.	6 0
	£3-12-4

Blue brocate
white

black brocate

Cloth A106 2yd 10" = 2 3/8 yd
@ 38/6

Satin 2yds 5" = 2 1/4 yd
Vilene 2yds @ 2/2½ yd
Making 80/-

Cloth 2yds 10" = 2 3/8 yd @ 38/6	£4 . 11 . 6
Satin 2yd 5" = 2 1/4 yds @ 3/3	£0 7 4
Vilene 2yd @ 2/2½ yd	£0 4 5
Making 80/-	£4 . 0 . 0
BRAID APPROX 26/-	£9 . 3 . 3d
	10 4 3

CLASSIC
PADDINGTON
STREET. W.1.
CLASSIC
ACCONIS
CONFECTIONERS
UNITED
TOBACCONISTS
94 BAKER ST

'The exterior was done over one weekend, executed by the members of The Fool and a few art students; the interior murals were executed by myself and Simon during the following three or four weeks. During the same period Yosha and I designed all the clothing, chose the materials and had them manufactured from my fashion sketches. We did all the designing, pattern-making and sewing ourselves, except, of course, the commercially manufactured lines. For those we just made the samples. The usual course of action was to put a design sketch on paper, make the pattern, buy the fabric and sew the garment. In some instances we hand-silkscreened our own fabric designs.

'I don't know why Apple was labelled a boutique, as it was intended to be more of a cultural centre with books and musical instruments, art shows, lectures, poetry readings, music nights etc. etc. Unfortunately the whole thing was badly managed, which had nothing to do with The Fool. We were just the creative idea people and had our hands full painting and designing.'

Whatever people thought of The Fool and their clothes, everyone agreed that the mural was magnificent, a real work of art that captured everyone's imagination.

On 7 December 1967 the Apple shop was opened with a big launch party. Present among the many guests were Cilla Black, Pattie Boyd and two Beatles: John, in a white jacket, black polo-neck and trousers, and George, resplendent in a green striped suit (collar cut very particularly) and a green neckerchief to finish the effect off. Very Dandy. The Fool entered the shop in their court jester costumes, banging on tambourines and playing flutes. Both Beatles ate apples.

The shop operated on two floors. In the basement they sold The Fool's clothes and other clothing items. (Just before the shop closed for good, they were planning to invite the famous designer Ossie Clark to produce a range.) On the ground floor there was jewellery, beads, Red Indian necklaces, Moroccan wedding belts, exotic musical instruments and a handful of selected albums by acts such as Blood Sweat and Tears.

At first, the shop showed every sign of prospering.

'The boutique gave every indication of being an enormous success', Shotton recalled in the book *John Lennon: In My Life*. 'The shop was packed throughout the Christmas season, and the merchandise seemed to fly off the shelves almost as fast as we could replenish the stock. The trouble was that so much of it seemed to disappear from the premises without benefit of a cash transaction. Our turned-on, tuned-in staff was not only loath to apprehend shoplifters – for fear of being unhip – but also felt few scruples about helping themselves to whichever goods happened to catch their fancy.'

This is a perception about the Apple shop that has travelled down the years – that its inability to turn a profit was mainly caused by the staff stealing the goods. One person who utterly denies this claim is Delilah, who worked at the shop in 1968. She told me: 'As far as I remember it, we were all very excited to be working there and really felt we were part of something special, that what The Beatles were creating was something we all felt a part of, and we wouldn't have done anything to spoil that. There is a thing on Wikipedia that makes that claim and it really annoys me.'

Yet by January 1968 the shop was starting to lose money. Many felt that Shotton's skills in running a supermarket did not translate into running a unique operation like the Apple shop. That was when The Beatles turned to John Lyndon.

John Lyndon was born and raised in Norwich. He attended the London Academy of Music and Dramatic Acts and through his various contacts met Brian Epstein in 1963. After an introductory lunch, Epstein offered him a job at NEMS as a stage production manager.

It would be his job to produce shows for Epstein's ever-growing stable of acts. Lyndon joined the firm on the day The Beatles' manager moved to London full-time, and worked closely with Cilla Black and Gerry Marsden, the front man of Gerry and the Pacemakers. (Marsden was also managed by Epstein and is famous for hits such as 'Ferry Cross the Mersey' and 'I Like It'.) He also travelled around

OPPOSITE The original, startling mural that The Fool had painted on the side of the shop and which was subsequently removed at the insistence of the shop's landlords, Portman Estates.

FOLLOWING PAGES · LEFT TO RIGHT Crowds outside the Apple shop. The model Twiggy at the party to launch the Apple shop on 5 December 1967.

CLASSIC
Borough of St. Marylebone
PADDINGTON
STREET. W.1.
apple
apple
CLASSIC

OPPOSITE Pattie Boyd's sister Jenny was an early employee at the Apple shop (above).

Europe with the Bee Gees. However, Lyndon found some people within the NEMS empire not to his liking, which is why in January 1968 he accepted an offer to produce a show at the MIDEM Music Festival in the south of France.

'I took a break one day,' he told me, 'and I was sitting on the beach ..., and all of a sudden there was a tap on my shoulder and it was Peter Brown [management assistant to The Beatles] with Paul [McCartney]. And Peter said to me, "Paul has asked me to come down here with him because he wants to ask you something." He said, "Would you go in and have a look at Apple retail for us." My very first job when I left school was to become a bespoke tailor at a place called Ridley's in Norwich. I said I don't think I want to put my foot in that pool [Apple] any more. At the time, you see, I was intending to give it all up. ... So I said no to the Apple job initially.'

Lyndon's plan was to accept an offer from America to work at the DesiLu studios, an operation set up by popular entertainers Desi Arnaz and Lucille Ball and busy producing TV hits such as *Star Trek*. Unfortunately, before he could travel there, Lyndon's mother suffered a stroke, and he rushed to be near her. With only the Apple job on the table, Lyndon took over the shop in early February, just as The Beatles were departing for Rishikesh in India to study transcendental meditation with the Maharishi.

Lyndon's first call was to a window dresser named Ken Brown, who had helped decorate Brian Epstein's house in Belgravia. The two men went to look at the Apple shop and, although they liked the shop's atmosphere and vibe, they knew many changes had to be made.

'When I arrived, I could see that the shop certainly was not designed to make any money. The atmosphere and the whole idea of it were great. But a lot of it was daft', Lyndon recalls.

For instance, the changing rooms had no dividers. People were scared to go in and strip off in front of others just to try on Apple clothing. Dividers were quickly installed.

Lyndon's staff at the time consisted of two girls, Jean and Hilary, and a man called Caleb, whom Lyndon nicknamed 'Brown Rice Boy' as his other job in life was to read Tarot cards to any interested Apple staff. Lyndon also brought in a PA named Nicola Lydell (who would later marry the writer Peter Mayle). One of Apple's earliest staff members was Jenny Boyd, the sister of George Harrison's wife, the famous model Pattie Boyd. By the time Lyndon arrived, however, she had left the shop.

As far as John was concerned, 'There was very little on sale there the band could make money from.'

The shop did carry some intriguing items, though. There were the Apple bed sheets, for example, made in white, with the image of a boy printed on one side and a girl on the other. These were designed by the artist Martin Battersby, whom Lyndon described as 'one of the great *trompe-l'oeil* painters of the last century'. (*Trompe-l'oeil* is a painting style that focuses on hyper-realism and visual illusion.)

Battersby worked out of his studio in Brighton and also produced Apple underpants, which were white with an apple placed at the front. The shop sold dressing gowns in different colours, whose designs gave the impression of a chessboard. Pottery made by Peter Fluck was also on sale. (Fluck would later gain fame and notoriety as one of the driving forces behind the very popular 1980s' TV show *Spitting Image*.)

'Very kinky and twisted', Lyndon now says of Fluck's work.

Not long after Lyndon assumed control, the large mural that The Fool had painted on the outside wall started to become an issue. Many shop owners and residents in the area started complaining. But, contrary to other published accounts of the shop, Lyndon is keen to stress that it was not Westminster Council who demanded its removal but Portman Estates, the company who owned the building's freehold.

'Portman Estates to this day own the freehold on that building', Lyndon says. 'And it was Portman Estates that threatened to issue a writ to return the building to its status quo. Westminster Council had nothing to do with the mural being removed; it was Portman Estates that said "You have got to get rid of this." They said that, and I brought in some contractors and they painted it white one Sunday. I thought it was criminal. I thought it was a landmark of our times.'

OPPOSITE Martin Battersby's original Apple underpants. Battersby also designed Apple boy and girl bed sheets.

The Fool's clothing was also proving to be troublesome. It was costly to produce and not selling anywhere near the numbers required to make it financially viable. What Lyndon needed was a big-selling item to offset the losses. He and his team came up with a design for a hipster trouser in linen, which was produced in turquoise, pink, beige and off-white. They manufactured about 400 pairs and sold them at £7.

The trousers sold well and began to generate the funds needed. 'The shop had started to pick up, we had started to take money', Lyndon recalls.

The shop's customers, he noted, tended to be tourists from all over the world. 'Everyone around the world knew about the shop', he states. But despite this huge potential market, Lyndon reveals it was a constant struggle to extract money from his masters.

'I could never get the money out of them', he says. 'Although I was given carte blanche to do all sorts of things – which I did – the administrative side was always a nightmare.'

Lyndon can recall two Indian saleswomen approaching him during his time at the shop with imported goods from their country which he knew would sell extremely well. Yet Apple's reluctance to hand over money ensured that they both went and found success with other retail shops.

In July, Lyndon was called to a meeting at the new Apple offices in Savile Row. Present were Lyndon, all The Beatles and Yoko Ono. The subject was the shop's future. As talk began, the subject of a recent article was brought up.

'I was in the room in the day they decided to give it away', Lyndon states. 'John Peel wrote an article in the *Melody Maker,* and this article talked about "Jewish rag merchants", and that was always a sore point to John. Yoko said to John, "John, you are not a Jewish rag merchant", and then she said, "Give it away." Well, it is very easy for someone to say "Give away £300,000" – which today would be about £2 million – when it isn't their money to give away.

'But she was the one that said, "Give it away, you are not a Jewish rag merchant." This was in a meeting with the four boys, Yoko and myself, and no one has ever written that. Ringo couldn't care less, George kept going in and out, it was Paul trying to hold it all together, and the minute John thought that giving it away was a splendid idea, Paul was defeated. That is what happened. John did not say, "Give it away." Paul did not say, "Give it away." It was Yoko, and every book has got that wrong.'

John Peel's article appeared in the *Melody Maker* dated 27 July 1968, which means that The Beatles would actually have seen it on 22 July. In his article Peel did not call the band 'Jewish rag merchants'. (George Harrison did that in a later interview with the Jewish writer Ray Coleman.) Peel simply asked what The Beatles were doing surrounding themselves with accountants and businessmen. What did that have to do with the counterculture? Stung by this observation, and keen to be considered hipper than hip, they decided there was no better way to placate the anti-capitalist brigade than by giving away everything in the Apple shop for nothing.

Even so, Lyndon could not believe that the band would implement the idea. 'I couldn't believe it when they said they were going to give everything away, and I didn't believe it until the night The Beatles and Yoko arrived at the shop to take what they wanted.'

Ironically, Lyndon adds, it was Yoko who took the biggest bag away, although Lennon, in particular, loved ransacking the place. It brought the Teddy Boy in him back out for an airing.

'The night before we all went in and took what we wanted,' he recalled. 'It was great, it was like robbing. We took everything we wanted home.'

The next day the first customer in was told to put his money away, that everything in the shop was now free. The word soon spread, and hundreds of people descended on the shop, including a BBC news team. Significantly, they interviewed a young teenage boy and asked him if he had ever shopped at Apple. 'Nah,' he replied, 'it is too expensive.'

Lyndon is in agreement with his young critic. 'I mean, some of the clothes you could have got a Dougie Millings suit for the price.'

OPPOSITE A typical London girl admiring the Apple front window. Many customers grumbled initially about the price of the clothing.

ABOVE AND RIGHT On 31 July 1968 The Beatles sanctioned the giving away of all goods, before closing down the shop. The previous night the band, plus wives and girlfriends, had raided the shop themselves. Here the crowd show off their free goodies while two policemen also get in on the act.

OPPOSITE Crowds gathering outside the shop on the last day of its existence.

CLASSIC
PADDINGTON
STREET, W.1.
apple

For Derek Taylor, then working at Apple as a PR man, the sight of people fighting over the stock was quite upsetting. 'The giving away of the clothing brought out the worst in people that I dread to see', he wrote. 'Cabbies were grabbing Kaftans and capes and silk-ruffled shirts off the rails – "I want this" and "I want that." I thought it was one of the ugliest things I had ever heard of, this giving away of the clothes.'

Typically, John Lyndon refused to take anything.

'I thought the whole thing was nuts. I was absolutely gobsmacked by it. I came back to the office after that first meeting and I remember telling Nicola [Lydell], "They are going to give this all away." She said, "Well let's take everything while we can." I said, "I don't want anything from it." And I didn't. I didn't want a single thing. I felt I had been given a rough hand. I never received even one penny of commission. I worked very hard and did everything straightforwardly and with honesty. I saw all these rip-off merchants coming in and fleecing everything, and I thought, "Oh no, I don't want to be like them."'

And he never was.

Despite the fluctuating fortunes of the Apple shop on Baker Street, The Beatles ploughed on with the opening of a second clothing venture, called Apple Tailoring. Over the past year, 1967–8, they had been very taken with the work of the designer John Crittle, an Australian who with Neil Winterbotham, Alan Holston and Tara Browne had opened Dandie Fashions at Kensington Mews in Ocotber 1966 and relocated to 161 King's Road in 1967.

Tara Browne died in a car crash in 1966 and was immortalised by Lennon and McCartney in their song 'A Day in the Life'. Despite his passing, Dandie Fashions prospered. As Richard Lester (the author of *Boutique London*, not the film director) writes: 'The clothes were specifically designed with the modern dandy in mind – brocade, velvet, tapestry – a meeting of stage costume and bespoke tailoring that pre-empted the blurring of divisions between form and function and between genders of the Glam Rock era to come.'

In anticipation of the company joining forces with the Apple organisation, Neil Aspinall joined as a director of Dandie Fashions in February 1968. The idea was to appeal to an older, more affluent market than its counterpart on Baker Street.

Interviewed at the time, Crittle said, 'The Beatles' dress sense is quietening down now, like everyone else. They all went mad last year, but now they are all coming back to a normal way of life. We won't get teenyboppers here, because prices will be too high for them. We're pushing velvet jackets and the Regency look, although the Beatles put forward plenty of suggestions. They have pretty far ahead ideas actually. We're catering mainly for pop groups, personalities and turned-on swingers.

'The teenagers seem too frightened to come in, even though they know this is the Beatles' place. Maybe it's because the place is too elegant and too expensive.'

As the shop was readied for opening, on 11 May 1968, John and Paul flew to New York to formally launch Apple in the States. The week before (the night of 3/4 May, estimates Mark Lewisohn), John and Yoko Ono had begun their famous love affair. Such was the effect of this relationship on John that, tellingly, for the next few months he would tend to wear either all-white or all-black clothing. Of all The Beatles, John seemed to be the one who used clothes most to send out signals – obscure signals maybe, but signals all the same – to the outside world. Maybe the love he felt for Yoko presaged in him the desire for a new start, a new adventure, and the purity of that love and their feelings would be represented by his white clothing. The Apple Tailoring opening party – again attended by John and George and not the others – is famous for being the first public event that John and Yoko attended together.

Apple Tailoring was not the only business operating on the premises. Down in the basement Apple Hair was opened. The man in charge was Leslie Cavendish. Cavendish was now well established in Beatle World as Numero Uno hairdresser. This fortunate turn of events had begun that day at Vidal Sassoon's when he agreed to Jane Asher's request for him to cut her 'boyfriend's hair'.

Not long after this relationship started, Cavendish received a phone call from Beatle PR man Derek Taylor. Could he come in and cut his hair? He had heard good things from Paul. Cavendish went to the Apple offices, now located at

ABOVE George and John at the launch party for Apple Tailoring on 23 May 1968 at the Arethusa Club in the King's Road. Later on, John posed outside the shop at 161 King's Road with his new girlfriend, Yoko Ono, lurking in the background. No one yet realised her role in his life, and so the paparazzi missed a real exclusive.

Civil and Theatrical
Apple Tailoring
by John Crittle

OPPOSITE AND ABOVE Shots of the Apple Tailoring shop, which was run by John Crittle, the Australian designer and father of the ballet dancer Darcey Bussell. Downstairs Leslie Cavendish ran the Apple hair salon, designed to attract an exclusive 'in crowd'.

FOLLOWING PAGES Such was the intensity of their relationship that John and Yoko both tended to wear either white or black, to signify their romantic union. Previously John had dressed like a Beatle; now he dressed to be in harmony with his new love.

LeVI ST

Wigmore Street, and met Taylor, thus starting a relationship that would lead to him assuming responsibility for George and John's hair as well. Ringo's hair was usually looked after by Maureen, his wife, but when she couldn't attend to it, Cavendish stepped in.

By September 1967 Cavendish was firmly ensconced as the band's favourite hairdresser, which is why he was invited on to the *Magical Mystery Tour* film, which began shooting on 11 September 1967. His workload was hardly demanding, and Cavendish spent two enjoyable weeks driving around England's countryside with the most famous band in the world.

The group then returned to London, and editing on the film began. As 1967 came to an end, Cavendish received a call from John asking him to come to Wigmore Street and cut his hair. When Cavendish arrived, he was shown through to an office, where John was sitting with a young Japanese woman. Cavendish automatically assumed that John's visitor was a journalist. He had no idea that this was Yoko Ono.

'Because of the way his hair was,' Cavendish recalls, 'which was quite long, it wouldn't take long to cut it. Now John was always one of those guys who kept asking why. You would say something and he would say, "Why?" Here he is talking to Yoko, who I think is some journalist, and he keeps saying "Why?" She was talking to him about art, and he kept saying "Why?" and I thought to myself, "This is interesting, I'm going to make this haircut last." I was fascinated. He kept pounding away, and he would get angry. "I don't understand that, why?" She was doing an exhibition at the Indica which was full of clever ideas.

'Like, when you walked in, you had to sign your name, which after a while became a tapestry – that kind of thing. Now for John Lennon this was really fucking his mind up. He is supposed to know everything and he is engrossed in her. He is a songwriter, and he is getting something that his fellow musicians have never seen. You could see why he would be so attracted to her. It was her mind, and I am sure that was the attraction.'

As for Harrison, Cavendish warmed to him. 'The thing about George', he later recalled, 'is that he never said much, but when he did say something it was always worth listening to.'

In early 1968 Paul began talking to Cavendish about setting up an exclusive hair salon where they and their contemporaries in the arts field could get their hair cut privately. The chance to work under the Apple Tailoring shop on the King's Road, attending to an highly exclusive clientele, was irresistible. Cavendish joined the Apple payroll.

The first rule he was given was that the salon could not advertise, especially on the street outside. Everyone knew that Leslie Cavendish was The Beatles' hairdresser, and the band didn't want to attract legions of fans to the location.

Apple gave Leslie £3,000 to decorate the salon. He bought blue and white Italian floor tiles from a shop in Pimlico named Casa Pupo, and some mirror balls. Two chairs were installed in front of mirrors, and the walls were painted white with blue edges. Leslie also employed a young manicurist named Marianne and occasionally, in exchange for a haircut, brought in a young busker who would serenade the waiting customers with his acoustic guitar.

One of those customers – who included over the years Keith Moon, Peter Cook, Nina Simone and Robin and Barry Gibb – was a journalist named Caroline Boucher. Boucher worked for *Disc and Music Echo*, and during a haircut asked Leslie who had the best hair out of the Beatles. Walking right into her trap, Leslie told her that George's was the strongest, then Paul's, and then John's. He added that, if anyone was going to go bald, it would be John.

(If we recall Dezo Hoffmann's earlier account of being shouted down by John in Miami in 1964 after capturing him on film with his hairline showing, then baldness may well have been a real concern for Lennon.)

Not long after, quite early in the morning, Leslie's phone rang. It was Derek Taylor, asking Leslie why *Disc* were running a story that John Lennon was going bald.

Mortified, Leslie's next call was from Lennon himself. Before he could speak, Leslie was babbling down the line about how sorry he was and that it had just been a mistake. Lennon cut him off. 'Don't worry,' the Beatle said ruefully, 'I've been misquoted a few times in the press myself.'

Although the salon remained profitable, Apple Tailoring was struggling. The market they had hoped to appeal to remained unimpressed, while the band's younger fans had no use for such a venture.

In fact, it is quite telling that by mid-1967 the group's coverage in magazines such as *Fab 208* was dwindling considerably. The admission of using LSD, the move away from playing live to screaming girl fans, the desire for much more privacy from the press and the band's increasing interest in such esoteric things as meditation left the way wide open for others to grab the coverage once granted to the Fabs ...

Meet The Monkees, a manufactured band designed to be America's own ... Beatles. It was they who now started topping the polls and who were given huge coverage.

As for The Beatles, they were lucky to get one page. In one of the magazine's last ever interviews with Beatleworld, the DJ Annie Nightingale interviewed John and Yoko. She subtly complains about being spoken at for hours by the couple – 'John then went into a long discourse about how he likes women's clothes, used to do dress designing, and how John and Yoko might put on a fashion show' – and does not hide her pleasure at getting out of the building. Such sentiments would have been unthinkable just two years previously.

In the end John Crittle quit the shop and returned to Australia, where he died in 2000. Leslie retained the salon and kept cutting Beatle hair right until the end. When they relinquished the property, he retained the salon and was always astonished that Apple never asked for any money back from him. He worked at the salon until 1972, when he went into clothes retailing.

If Crittle had been unable to make Apple Tailoring a success, he had been spot-on about one thing. The Beatles clothes had calmed down. The hope of the Summer of Love had been fatally undermined by the escalation of the Vietnam War and the stark reality of the horrors being committed in that part of the world.

Fancy clothing no longer seemed relevant, and by the time of the *Magical Mystery Tour* film the band were back to smart, casual clothing, with some typically individual touches. One thinks mainly of Paul's colourful Fair Isle tank-top sweater, which an aunt knitted for him, and the feather (literally) in John's hat. Badges also seem to be popular, a trend that had begun in the summer of 1967. John's would say things like 'Down With Pants' or 'Sword Swallower'. Some of the badges came from fans. An American woman named Lesley Samuels visited The Beatles in July 1967 and gave them a handful of American badges. In 1968, when John travelled to New York with Paul to launch Apple, he wore a huge white badge on his jacket.

The band's casual but smart clothing look continued through 1968 and is in much evidence in the video films for the 'Hey' songs – 'Hey Jude' and 'Hey Bulldog'. Particularly striking in the latter are George Harrison's corduroy boots, especially when one recalls a little note in an issue of *Beatles Monthly* from 1964 which says that as a young boy George had explored the possibility of creating a corduroy shoe. He was laughed out of all the Liverpool cobblers he visited. Now here he was wearing his own exclusive pair. Because that was the thing about being a Beatle – whatever your dream was, someone was always willing to make it come true.

In March 1969 John declared he would be growing his hair for peace, thus negating the need for Leslie Cavendish's scissors. He did so at a time when Apple now operated out of its most prestigious and famous address: 3 Savile Row.

This was the tiny London street made famous by the original Regency dandy, Beau Brummell. Brummell used a tailor on Savile Row, and such was his influence that soon most of London was descending on the street. Before long the street had become exclusive: the place where royalty and the upper classes went to have their suits made. Discretion and a very British politeness still pervade the street. But at some point tradition must meet the real world.

Apple had money and power and influence from a source – music – not normally recognised by Savile Row. Their landing on the street was a turning point.

One of the main directors of the company was Peter Brown, who at the time was romantically involved with a very hip tailor named Tommy Nutter. With backing

FOLLOWING PAGES Paul and Linda marry on 12 March 1969 at Marylebone Registry Office. Paul's brother and best man, Mike McGear, is on the right.

money provided by Cilla Black and her husband, Bobby, Nutter now opened up on Savile Row. You could hear the snorts of derision for miles around. But Nutter was ambitious, a quiet man but with determination fuelling his dreams. According to Nik Cohn, Tommy Nutter 'was a comely youth from Edgware, and what made him intriguing was that he had set up shop with no qualifications of any kind, beyond the sweetness of his smile'.

The year before he had worked in the Burlington Arcade, where he had seemed destined to remain, until he made contact with Cilla, probably though Peter Brown. Nutter had one thing on his side that his rivals didn't – the cutter Edward Sexton. Considered one of the greatest cutters of his time, Sexton ensured that Nutter's suits were modish but always highly elegant. His suits had classic shapes and styles but with new ideas thrown into them. Thus the lapels on Nutter's suits expanded, and so did the jackets. But he also dared to dream, often matching a dog-tooth check with a Prince of Wales check and making a success of it all.

It was Nutter's white suit that Lennon wore when he married Yoko Ono in Gibraltar on 20 March 1968, and it was his suits that the band took to wearing. As the band were now spending a lot of their time on business affairs, it seems appropriate that they should adopt suits at this juncture in their lives. It seemed to be their way of saying, 'Pop is big business now. We thought it was all about love, but it's not, it's about cash.'

They certainly needed a new look. The clothes they sport in their *Let It Be* film (made in January 1969) show a band whose dress sense matches their fading spirits. Arguing over direction and with everyone except John highly annoyed by Yoko's presence at every session, the band's listlessness is reflected in their drab clothing. Unshaven a lot of the time, it is as if even their wardrobe doesn't know which way to go now.

Tommy Nutter's suits provided a welcome diversion on the sartorial front, and it was these that the band – apart from George, who opted for denim – wore for the cover of *Abbey Road*, up there with *Sgt Pepper* as one of the most iconic album covers ever.

The band is shown marching across Abbey Road's zebra crossing, but they are apart now. John, in particular, looks like he is furiously striding away from the others. He was with Yoko now, and by his own admission she had taken the place 'of that old gang of mine'.

Worse, The Beatles were seriously arguing among themselves over management and financial matters. McCartney wanted to go one way; the other three disagreed. It is telling, then, that in the last few pictures of the band Paul is clean-shaven and the others wear beards. At the last ever Beatle photo shoot – at John's house in Tittenhurst – Lennon looks like a ghost, a spectral presence. It is the most disturbing shot of Lennon, as if he was about to disappear into the background. George and Ringo look completely uninterested as well, with only McCartney – as ever – trying to inject some energy into the band he loved so much.

In all previous Beatle photo shoots the band had instinctively moved towards one another. They were a gang, who looked and spoke the same language. But now they were moving away from each other, miles apart.

And in all Beatle photo shoots clothes are highly important. There is a sense of pride in their look, another way of declaring to the world the quality of their ideas and imagination. But now all the colour was gone, the clothes put into mothballs and the wardrobe door firmly shut.

It would never be opened again ... until now.

OPPOSITE Despite the smart suit and smiles, McCartney was now fighting the other Beatles over management issues, and the thought of losing the band he adored was killing him.

ABOVE Ringo finally gives in and grows his hair long. Here, with his wife, Maureen, the couple look very '70s as they go to board their plane. Ringo's hair and beard were matched by John and George.

OPPOSITE John performs with Yoko's Plastic Ono Band, again with the all-white look.

EAMONN
PEACE
BAGISM

OPPOSITE On April Fool's Day John and Yoko sat in a big bag before appearing on Eamonn Andrews's *Today* programme. (Andrews sits on the bed behind them.) Yoko and world peace were now far more important to John than the band. Thanks to his close relationship with Brian Jones (another snazzy dresser, whose style would have attracted the well-dressed Beatles), John also appeared with Yoko, dressed as clown and wizard respectively, on the Rolling Stones' *Rock 'n' Roll Circus* TV special, filmed at the Internel Studios, Stonebridge Park, near Wembley, in December 1968. They also attended the press conference for the show, with Jones and Eric Clapton.

RIGHT Long hair and denim was now George's favourite look, as he and Pattie travelled to Nice in September 1969.

ABOVE AND OPPOSITE John with Hippie hairstyle in 1969. During this period Paul symbolically stayed clean-shaven and quite smart as the two former friends bitterly tore into each other.

ABOVE The tailor Tommy Nutter, who designed suits worn by three of the band (Paul, John and Ringo) for their famous *Abbey Road* album cover (right).
With the band now spending most of their time in business meetings, they would often be seen in suits, an acknowledgement that pop was now big money and that the 1967 dream of 'All You Need Is Love' had faded far away.

RIGHT Another famous Beatles sleeve. The Fabs ending their career – as they began – in suits.

OPPOSITE The band's last gig famously took place on the roof of their office at 3 Savile Row, on 30 January 1969. The band had always previously appeared in matching outfits for live shows, and the fact that each member of the band was now dressing to please himself demonstrates how fragile The Beatles had become. The end was nigh.

The Beatles on Apple

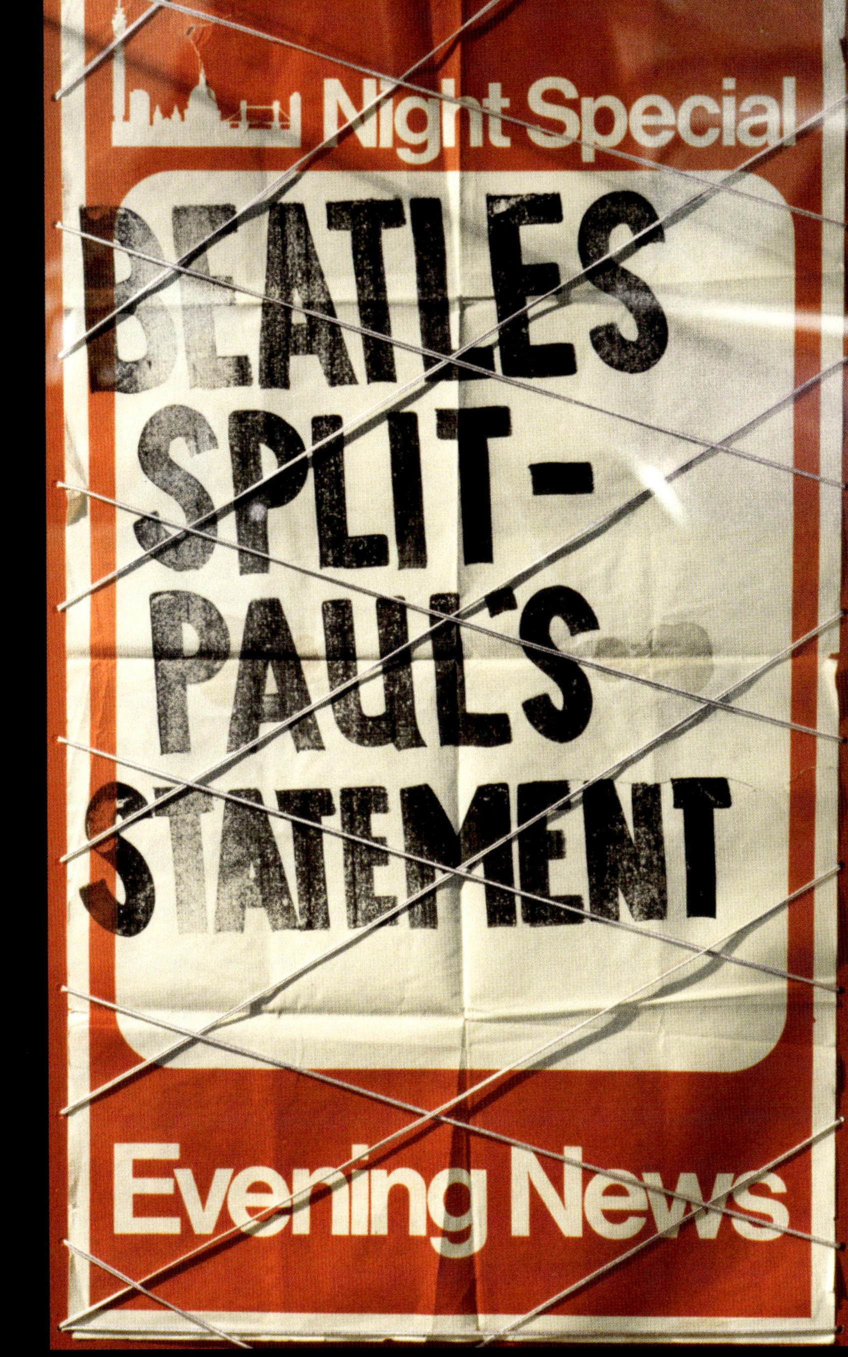
Night Special
BEATLES SPLIT-PAUL'S STATEMENT
Evening News

FAB THANKS

DEDICATION

This one is for you Mark Lewisohn, and for you Simon Wells – both of you Fab beyond words. It is also dedicated to the memory of Tom Chandler (1991–2011). I hope you found peace.

To Andrew Hansen, Philippa Hurd, Supriya Malik and everyone at Prestel; my agent, David Luxton, and this book's fine editor, Matthew Taylor; to the Getty folk – Rick Mayston (COYS), Martina Oliver, Pat Lyttle and Caroline Theakston; and to those who sat down and shared their memories and time and expertise with me – Delilah, Claudio Rossi, Julian Carr, Walter Smith, Billy Hatton, Steve and his partner at The Beatle Shop, Liverpool, Colin and Sylvia Hall, Tony Bramwell, Ben Stagg, Simon Hayes, John Pearse, Johnny Chandler, Mark Baxter, Mr Freeman, Marijke, Christopher Makris, Leslie Cavendish, Jon Savage, Spencer Leigh, Mark Lewisohn (WLBE), Simon Wells (OFR) and especially John Lyndon, for his generosity.

PICTURE CREDITS

All images have been provided by Getty images with the exception of those in italics

Page 2 BIPS/Stringer/Hulton Archive; **p. 7** Michael Ochs Archives/Stringer; **p. 8** K & K Ulf Kruger OHG/Contributor; **p. 11** Haywood Magee/Stringer; **p. 12** Michael Ochs Archives/Stringer; **p. 14** Astrid Kirchherr – K & K/Contributor; **p. 15 Above:** Jürgen Vollmer/Contributor; **Right:** V&A Images/Contributor; **Far right:** Keystone Features/Stringer; **p. 16** Jürgen Vollmer/Contributor; **p. 18** Keystone/Stringer; **p. 21** Keystone Features/Stringer; **p. 22** Michael Ochs Archives/Stringer; **p. 24** Jürgen Vollmer/Contributor; **p. 25 Left:** Jürgen Vollmer/Contributor; **Right:** Astrid Kirchherr – K & K/Contributor; **p. 27** Astrid Kirchherr – K & K/Contributor; **p. 28** Keystone/Stringer; **p. 30** Mark and Colleen Hayward/Contributor; **p. 31** Evening Standard/Stringer; **p. 32** Astrid Kirchherr – K & K/Contributor; **p. 33 Above:** Hulton Archive/Staff; **Below:** K & K Ulf Kruger OHG/Contributor; **p. 36** Keystone/Stringer; **p. 37 Left:** Michael Ochs Archives/Stringer; **Right:** Keystone/Stringer; **p. 38** Terrence Spencer/Contributor; **p. 41** Tom Hanley/Contributor; **p. 42** Chris Ware/Stringer; **p. 45** Astrid Kirchherr – K & K/Contributor; **p. 46** Astrid Kirchherr – K & K/Contributor; **p. 49 Above left:** Michael Ochs Archives/Stringer; **Above right:** Express/Stringer; **Below:** Popperfoto/Contributor; **p. 50** Left: Max Scheler – K & K/Contributor; **Right:** Keystone/Stringer; **p. 51** Keystone-France/Contributor; **p. 52** Michael Ochs Archives/Stringer; **p. 54 Above:** Popperfoto/Contributor; **Right:** Popperfoto/Contributor; **p. 56** Fiona Adams/Contributor; **p. 58** Paul Popper/Popperfoto/Contributor; **p. 60 Above left & right:** Evening Standard/Stringer; **Below:** Keystone/Stringer; **p. 61** Peter Hall/Contributor; **p. 62** Popperfoto/Contributor; **p. 63** Michael Ochs Archives/Stringer; **p. 64** David Redfern/Staff; **p. 65** Fox Photos/Stringer; **p. 66** Paul Popper/Popperfoto/Contributor; **p. 67** Fox Photos/Stringer; **p. 68** Central Press/Stringer; **p. 69** David Redfern/Staff; **p. 72** David Farrell/Contributor; **p. 73 Left:** Evening Standard/Stringer; **Right:** Popperfoto/Contributor; **p. 74** Max Scheler – K & K/Contributor; **p. 75 Above left to right:** Michael Ochs Archives/Stringer; **Below:** Sammlung Blaschke – K & K/Contributor; **p. 76 Above left:** Popperfoto/Contributor; **Above right:** Terrence Spencer/Contributor; **Below:** Michael Ochs Archives/Stringer; **p. 77** Paul Popper/Popperfoto/Contributor; **p. 78** John Rodgers/Contributor; **p. 79 Above:** Popperfoto/Contributor; **Below left:** Michael Ochs Archives/Stringer; **Below right:** Popperfoto/Contributor; **p. 80** Bob Gomel/Contributor; **p. 81** Jim Gray/Stringer; **p. 82** K & K Ulf Kruger OHG/Contributor; **p. 83** Evening Standard/Stringer; **p. 84** K & K Ulf Kruger OHG/Contributor; **p. 85** Michael Ochs Archives/Stringer; **p. 86** Express/Stringer; **p. 87** Max Scheler – K & K/Contributor; **p. 88** Michael Ochs Archives/Handout; **pp. 89–90** Michael Ochs Archives/Stringer; **p. 91 Above:** Bill Ray/Contributor; **Below:** New York Daily News Archive/Contributor; **p. 92** David Redfern/Staff; **p. 93** Evening Standard/Stringer; **p. 94 Left:** Larry Ellis/Stringer; **Right:** Evening Standard/Stringer; **p. 95** Michael Ochs Archives/Stringer; **p. 96** Keystone/Stringer; **pp. 97–98** Hulton Archive/Stringer; **p. 99** Roger Viollet Collection/Contributor; **p. 100 Left:** Express Newspapers/Stringer; **Right:** K & K Ulf Kruger OHG/Contributor; **p. 101 Left:** K & K Ulf Kruger OHG/Contributor; **Right:** Fiona Adams/Contributor; **p. 102 Above:** Takeyoshi Tanuma/Contributor; **Below:** Ron Howard/Contributor; **p. 103** Express/Stringer; **pp. 104–105** Wesley/Stringer; **p. 106** Cummings Archives/Contributor; **p. 107** Michael Ochs Archives/Stringer; **p. 108 Left:** Michael Ochs Archives/Handout; **Right:** George Stroud/Stringer; **p. 109** Terry Disney/Stringer; **p. 110** Keystone-France/Contributor; **p. 111 Left:** Chris Jackson/Staff; **Right:** Virginia Turbett/Contributor; **p. 113** John Pratt/Stringer; **p. 114** John Downing/Contributor; **p. 117 Above:** Watson/Stringer; **Below:** Les Lee/Stringer; **p. 118** Cummings Archives/Contributor; **p. 119 Left:** Marvin Lichtner/Contributor; **Right:** Keystone-France/Contributor; **p. 121** Michael Ochs Archives/Stringer; **pp. 124–125** John Downing/Contributor; **p. 126** Express/Stringer; **p. 129** *Courtesy: Paolo Hewitt;* **pp. 130–131** John Downing/Contributor; **p. 132** John Downing/Contributor; **p. 133 Above:** Hulton Archives/Stringer; **Below Left to Right:** Michael Putland/Contributor; Alexandra Wyman/Staff; Dave M. Benett/Contributor; **p. 134** Les Lee/Stringer; **p. 135** Cummings Archives/Contributor; **p. 136 Left:** Michael Ochs Archives/Stringer; **Right:** Ivan Keeman/Contributor; **pp. 137–139** Ivan Keeman/Contributor; **pp. 140–141** Victor Blackman/Stringer; **p. 142** Evening Standard/Stringer; **p. 143 Left:** Keystone-France/Contributor; **Right:** Cummings Archives/Contributor; **p. 144 Left:** Estate of Keith Morris/Contributor; **Right:** George Freston/Stringer; **p. 145 Above:** Express/Stringer; **Below left:** Ted West/Stringer; **Below right:** Keystone/Stringer; **p. 146 Left:** Cummings Archives/Contributor; Right: Keystone Features/Stringer; **p. 147** Hulton Archives/Stringer; **p. 148** Left: Manchester Daily Express/Contributor; **Right:** Jim Gray/Stringer; **p. 149 Left:** Keystone/Stringer; Right: Terry O'Neill/Contributor; **p. 150** Jim Gray/Stringer; **p. 151 Above:** Jim Gray/Stringer; **Below:** Keystone/Stringer; **pp. 152–153** Keystone-France/Contributor; **pp. 154–155** Wesley/Stringer; **p. 156** Larry Ellis/Stringer; **p. 157** Central Press/Stringer; **p. 159** Hulton Archive/Staff; **p. 160 Top left:** Michael Ochs Archives/Stringer; **Top right:** David Redfern/Staff; **Bottom left and right:** Ivan Keeman/Contributor; **p. 162 Left & Right:** Popperfoto/Contributor; **p. 163 Left:** Michael Ochs Archives/Stringer; **Right:** Jürgen Vollmer/Contributor; **p. 165** Keystone/Stringer; **p. 166** Popperfoto/Contributor; **p. 170 Top left to right:** Popperfoto/Contributor; **Bottom:** Dave Hogan/Stringer; **p. 171** Mark & Colleen Hayward/Contributor; **p. 173** Express/Stringer; **p. 174** Hulton Archive/Stringer; **p. 175** K & K Ulf Kruger OHG/Contributor; **p. 176** Michael Ochs Archives/Stringer; **p. 177** Michael Ochs Archives/Stringer; **p. 178 Left:** Harry Benson/Stringer; **Right:** Keystone Features/Stringer; **p. 179 Left:** Clive Limpkin/Stringer; **Right:** John Downing/Contributor; **p. 180** David Redfern/Staff; **p. 181 Left:** Keystone/Stringer; **Right:** David Redfern/Staff; **p. 182 Top:** Wesley/Stringer; **Bottom:** Andrew Maclear/Contributor; **p. 183** David Redfern/Staff; **p. 184** Keystone Features/Stringer; **p. 185** Tom Hanley/Contributor; **p. 186** Tom Hanley/Contributor; **p. 187** Tom Hanley/Contributor; **p. 188** Tom Hanley/Contributor; **p. 189** Central Press/Stringer; **p. 190 Left:** George Stroud/Stringer; **Right:** Michael Ochs Archives/Handout; **p. 191** Keystone/Stringer; **p. 193** C. Maher/Stringer; **p. 194** Stroud/Stringer; **p. 197** *Photo: Philippa Hurd;* **pp. 198–201** *Courtesy: John Lyndon;* **p. 202** Mike Barnes/Stringer; **p. 204** Fred Mott/Stringer; **p. 205** Pierre Manevy/Stringer; **p. 206 Left:** Mike Barnes/Stringer; **Right:** Cummings Archives/Contributor; **p. 207** Ted West/Stringer; **p. 209** *Photo: Supriya Malik;* **p. 211** Mike Barnes/Stringer; **p. 212 Top:** Wesley/Stringer; **Bottom:** Bob Aylott/Stringer; **p. 213** C. Maher/Stringer; **p. 215** M. McKeown/Stringer; **pp. 216–217** Andrew Maclear/Contributor; **p. 218** Popperfoto/Contributor; **p. 219** Central Press/Stringer; **pp. 222–223** Keystone/Stringer; **p. 224** John Rodgers/Contributor; **p. 226** George Stroud/Stringer; **p. 227** Evening Standard/Stringer; **p. 228 Top left:** Bob Aylott/Stringer; **Top right:** Keystone/Stringer; Bottom: Hulton Archive/Stringer; **p. 229** Manchester Daily Express/Contributor; **pp. 230–231** Tom Hanley/Contributor; **p. 232 Above:** Jones/Stringer; *Below: Courtesy – Paolo Hewitt;* **p. 233** Express/Stringer; **p. 234** Blank Archives/Contributor; **p. 235** Epics/Contributor; Endpapers: courtesy of John Lyndon.

REFERENCES

MAGAZINES

Beatles Monthly (1963–70)
Beatlefan (1978)
Fab 208 (1964–70)
Man About Town (1960–62)
Town (1962–68)
Rave (1964–70)

BOOKS

Keith Badman *The Beatles Off The Record* (Omnibus, London, 2000)
The Beatles *The Beatles Anthology* (Cassell, London, 2000)
Pete Best *Beatle! The Pete Best Story* (Plexus, London, 1985)
Pattie Boyd *Wonderful Tonight: George Harrison, Eric Clapton, and Me* (Harmony Books, New York, 2008)
Tony Bramwell *Magical Mystery Tours: My Life with The Beatles* (Robson Books, London, 2005)
Nik Cohn *Today There Are No Gentlemen: The Changes in Englishmen's Clothes Since the War* (Weidenfeld & Nicolson, London, 1971)
Ray Coleman *John Lennon* (Futura, London, 1985)
Ray Coleman *Brian Epstein: The Man Who Made The Beatles* (Viking, London, 1989)
Hunter Davies *The Beatles* (Heinemann, London, 1968)
Sean Egan *The Mammoth Book of The Beatles* (Robinson, London, 2009)
Brian Epstein *A Cellar Full of Noise* (Souvenir Press, London, 1964)
Debbie Geller *The Brian Epstein Story* (Faber and Faber, London, 2000)
Jonathan Gould *Can't Buy Me Love: The Beatles, Britain, and America* (Harmony Books, New York, 2007)
George Harrison *I, Me, Mine* (Genesis, Guildford, 1980)
Bill Harry *Mersey Beat: The Beginnings of The Beatles* (Omnibus, London, 1977)
Dezo Hoffmann *With The Beatles: The Historic Photographs of Dezo Hoffmann* (Omnibus, London, 1982)
Cynthia Lennon *John* (Hodder & Stoughton, London, 2005)
Richard Lester *Boutique London: A History: King's Road to Carnaby Street* (ACC Editions, Woodbridge, 2010)
Mark Lewisohn *The Complete Beatles Chronicle* (Pyramid Books, London, 1992)
Peter McCabe and Robert D. Schonfeld *Apple to the Core* (Sphere Books, London, 1972)
Barry Miles *Paul McCartney: Many Years From Now* (Vintage, London, 1998)
Andrew Loog Oldham *Stoned* (Secker & Warburg, London, 2000)
David Pritchard *The Beatles: An Oral History* (Stoddart, Toronto, 1999)
Bernhard Roetzel *Gentleman: A Timeless Fashion* (Könemann, Cologne, 1999)
Billy Shepherd *The True Story of The Beatles* (Beat Publications, London, 1964)
Pete Shotton and Nicholas Schaffner *John Lennon: In my Life* (Hodder & Stoughton, London, 1984)
Bruce Spizer *The Beatles' Story on Capitol Records* (Four Ninety-Eight Productions, New Orleans, 2000)
Steven D. Stark *Meet The Beatles: A Cultural History of the Band that Shook Youth, Gender, and the World* (Harper Collins, London, 2005)
Derek Taylor *Fifty Years Adrift (In An Open-Necked Shirt)* (Genesis, Guildford, 1984)
Jürgen Vollmer *From Hamburg to Hollywood* (Genesis, Guildford, 1997)
Jürgen Vollmer *The Beatles in Hamburg* (Schirmer/Mosel, Munich, 2004)
Simon Wells *The Beatles: 365 Days* (Abrams, New York, 2005)
Allan Williams *The Man Who Gave The Beatles Away* (Elm Tree Books, London, 1975)

PERSONAL REMINISCENCES

Tony Bramwell, Julian Carr, Leslie Cavendish, Delilah, Billy Hatton, Simon Hayes, Mark Lewisohn, Glenn Ludlow, John Lyndon, John Pearse, Walter Smith, Ben Stagg

INDEX

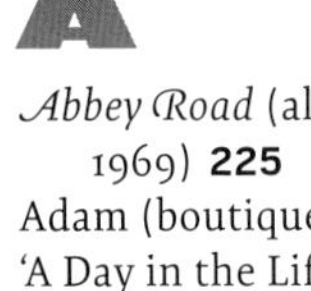

Abbey Road (album, 1969) 225
Adam (boutique) 71
'A Day in the Life' (song) 214
'All You Need Is Love' (song) 195
Altham, Keith 70
Anderson, Helen 59
Anello & Davide 39, 70
Apple 122, 195, 203, 208, 210, 214, 220, 221
Apple Tailoring 220, 221
Arnaz, Desi 208
Asher, Jane 172, 214
Aspinall, Neil 39, 115, 167, 214
Atlantic Records 47
Austin Reed (menswear) 71

B

Baker, Ginger 127
Ball, Lucille 208
Bardot, Brigitte 120, 164
Barrett, Syd 122
Barrymore, Michael 172
Baruch, Klaus 172
Battersby, Martin 208
BBC News 210
Beardsley, Aubrey 122
Beatles Monthly (magazine) 19, 55, 70, 115, 123, 127, 167, 221
Beatlefan (magazine) 167, 168
Bee Gees, The 208
Behrens, Val 169
Bermans (menswear) 127
Bernard, Andre 168
Best, Mona (Pete's mother) 23, 164
Best, Pete 23, 26, 29, 39, 47, 48, 164, 167
Beatle: The Pete Best Story 23
Billboard (magazine) 168
Bill Haley and the Comets 53
Black, Cilla 39, 203, 225
Blood, Sweat and Tears 203
Blue Caps, The 29
Bond, Graham 128
Boucher, Caroline 220
Boy Meets Girl 29
Boyd, Jenny 208
Boyd, Pattie 128, 203, 208
Bramwell, Tony 13, 29, 48, 53, 55, 71, 116, 120
Brando, Marlon 43
Brown, Ken 23, 208
Brown, Peter 208, 221, 225
Browne, Tara 214
Bruce, Jack 127
Brummell, George Bryan 'Beau' 17, 116, 221
Burberry 44
Burton's (menswear) 43
Bussell, Darcy 120
Byrne, Gay 168
Byron, Lord 116

C&A 29, 34
Cabaret Club, Liverpool 48
Capitol Records 168
Cardin, Pierre 57, 71
Carr, Julian 120, 122
Casa Pupo 220
Casbah Club, The 23
Cavendish, Leslie 120, 172, 214, 220, 221
Cavern Club, The 35, 44, 47
Charles, Caroline 59
Christian, David 122
Clapton, Eric 127
Clark, Dick 169
Clark, Ossie 203
Cleave, Maureen 53
Cocteau, Jean
Orpheus (film, 1950) 164
Cohen, Sheila 122
Cohn, Nik 9, 225
Coleman, Queenie 128
Coleman, Ray 43, 48, 53, 128
Cook, Peter 220
Cooper, Michael 127
Corbett, Bill 70
Craft Tailoring 47
Cream 127
Crittle, Andrea 120
Crittle, John 120, 122, 214, 221
Curtis, Tony 23, 26, 161, 167

Dakotas, The 169
Dandie Fashions 116, 120, 214
Darling (film, 1965) 71
Dave Clark Five 59
Davies, Hunter 19, 26, 57, 164
Dean, James 43
Delilah (Apple shop employee) 203
Dickins & Jones 59
Dior, Christian 44
Disc (magazine) 220
Dodd, Ken 168
Donis 71
Doran, Terry 122
Dorn, Beno 43, 47
Dudley, Paul 128
Dylan, Bob 59
The Freewheelin' (album, 1963) 59

Ed Sullivan Show, The 47, 168
Elizabeth II, queen of England 48
EMI 48
Epstein, Brian 39, 43, 44, 47, 48, 53, 57, 70, 123, 127, 128, 196, 203, 208
Esquires of Glasgow 70
Evans, Mal 71, 128
Evening Standard, The 53
Everett, Kenny 123

Fab 208 (magazine) 9, 34, 35, 55, 59, 70, 116, 120, 169
Fame, Georgie 120
Ferringo, Grace 169
Finch, Barry 128
Fisk, Ian 71
Flashing Fashion 127
Fluck, Peter 208
Fool, The 127, 128, 195, 196, 203, 208, 210
Four Tops, The 196
Fourmost, The 10
Freeman, Alan 70
Fury, Billy 19, 23, 53

Gee, Cecil 57
Gentle, Johnny 26
Gentry Male 71
Gerry and the Pacemakers 59, 70, 203
'Ferry Cross the Mersey' (song) 203
'I Like It' (song) 203
Getty, Paul Jnr. 120
Gibb, Barry 220
Gibb, Robin 220
Gibbs, Christopher 116
Girl Can't Help It, The (film, 1956) 29
Good, Jack 29
Goodman, Dennis 44
Gore, Jane Ormsby 116
Gould, Jonathan
Can't Buy Me Love 59
Graham Bond Organisation 128
Granada Television 44, 168
Granny Takes a Trip 116, 122
Greenaway, Kate 196

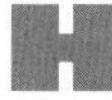

Hanmer, Bryce 195
Hard Day's Night, A (film, 1964) 71
Hardy, Françoise 120
Harlech, Lord 116
Harris, Julie 71
Harris, Wee Willie 53
Harrison, Harold (George's father) 19
Harry, Bill 17, 35
Hatton, Billy 10, 13, 43, 164
Hayes, George 43
Hayes, Simon 127, 128
Heath, Edward 57
Help! (film, 1965) 71
Hem and Fringe 71
Hendrix, Jimi 122, 196
'Hey Bulldog' (song) 221
'Hey Jude' (song) 221
His Clothes 71
Hitler, Adolf 167
Hoffmann, Dezo 70, 169, 220
Hollies, The
Evolution (album, 1967) 127
Holston, Alan 214
Hughes, Liz 35
Hung On You (boutique) 115, 116

I Was Lord Kitchener's Valet 71
Indra, The (club) 34
IT (magazine) 122

Jacaranda Club 23
Jacobs, Hyman 43
Jagger, Mick 9, 122, 127
Jay, Ivor 167
Jaywalkers, The 167
Johnny and the Moondogs 23
Johnson, Derek 115
Johnston, Shelagh 43
Jones, Brian 120, 122

Kaempfert, Bert 34
Kaiserkeller, The 26, 164
Kennedy, Pres. John F. 9
Kerouac, Jack
On the Road (1957) 13, 35
King Brothers 20
Kinks, The 10
Kirchherr, Astrid 26, 29, 57, 164, 167
Koger, Marijke 127, 128, 196, 203

Leeger, Josje (Yosha) 127, 128, 196, 203
Late Scene Extra 168
Leigh, Spencer 10

Leith Academy, Edinburgh **53**
Lennon, Cynthia **13, 34, 172**
John (2005) **127**
Lennon, Freddy (father) **13**
Lennon, Julia (mother) **13, 20**
Leonard's **169**
Lester, Dick
How I Won The War (film, 1967) **172**
Lester, Richard
Boutique London (2010) **214**
Let It Be (film, 1969) **221**
Levis, Carroll **23**
Lewis, Jerry Lee **34**
Lewisohn, Mark **20, 34, 44, 55, 57, 120, 195, 214**
Liberty **122**
Libro **53**
London Academy of Music and Dramatic Arts **203**
Ludlow, Glenn **70**
Lydell, Nicola **208, 214**
Lyndon, John **203, 208, 210, 214**

Magical Mystery Tour (film, 1967) **128, 220, 221**
Maharishi Mahesh Yogi **208**
Makris, Christopher **59, 169**
Marks and Spencer **26, 164, 195**
Marriott, Steve **17**
Marsden, Gerry **203**
Martin, George **48**
Marx Brothers **115**
Matthew, Brian **168**
Maxfield, Mike **169**
Mayle, Peter **208**
McCartney, Jim (father) **20, 35**
McCartney, Mary (mother) **20**
McCartney, Michael (brother) **20, 168**
McGowan, Cathy **55**
McKenna, Duncan **26**
Melka **48**
Melody Maker (magazine) **55, 210**
Mersey Beat (newspaper) **17, 35, 44**
MIDEM **208**
Miles, Barry
Paul McCartney: Many Years from Now **20, 161, 196**
Millings, Dougie **53, 55, 57, 70, 71, 115, 210**
Miracles, The **47**
Mister Carnaby **71**
Monkees, The **221**
Moon, Keith **127, 220**
Move, The **128**
Music Echo (magazine) **220**

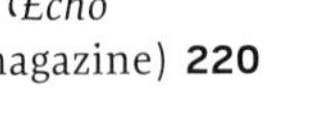

NEMS (record store) **39, 43, 203, 208**
New Musical Express (NME) **71, 115**
Newsweek **169**
New York Herald Tribune **168**
New York Times **169**
Nightingale, Annie **221**
Nutter, Tommy **221, 225**

Oldham, Andrew Loog **55**
Stoned **55**
Oldies But Goldies (album, 1966) **122**
Ono, Yoko **210, 214, 221**
Orbison, Roy **53**
Orrell Park Ballroom **48**

Parnes, Larry **23, 26**
Paul, John **71**
Paul's Boutique **71**
Pearse, John **122**
Peel, John **210**
'Penny Lane' (song) **123**
Poco **71**
Portman Estates **208**
Posthuma, Simon **127, 128, 196, 203**
Powe, Hector **53**
Presley, Elvis **23, 161**
Procul Harem **128**
Profumo, John **161**

Quant, Mary **59**
Quarrymen, The **20, 23**

Rainbows, The **23**
Rainey, Michael **116**
Rave (magazine) **70, 168, 195**
Ready Steady Go **55**
Rebel Without a Cause (film, 1955) **43**
Revolver (album, 1966) **122, 169**
Richard, Cliff **53**
Richards, Keith **127**
Ridley's of Norwich **208**
Robbins, Marty
'A White Sports Coat (And A Pink Carnation)' (song) **20**
Roberts, Chris **55**
Roger, Bunny **116, 120, 161**
Rolling Stones, The **55, 116, 120**
Rubber Soul (album, 1965) **169**
Rushdie, Salman **122**
Russell, Paul **168**

S

Samuels, Lesley **221**
Sartorial Executive **70**
Sartre, Jean-Paul **26**
Sassoon, Vidal **172**
Schlesinger, John **71**
Sexton, Edward **221**
Sgt. Pepper's Lonely Hearts Club Band (album, 1967) **116, 122, 123, 127, 172, 225**
'Sgt. Pepper's Lonely Hearts Club Band' (song) **115**
Shankar, Ravi **120**
'She Loves You' (song) **169**
Shepherd, Billy (Peter Jones) **17**
The True Story of the Beatles **9, 23, 35, 161, 167**
Shotton, Pete **13, 17, 20, 161, 195, 196**
Shotton, Pete and Nicholas Schaffner
In My Life **203**
Silver Beetles, The **23, 26**
Simone, Nina **220**
Sinatra, Frank **168**
Slade **34**
Slaver, James **57**
Small Faces, The **17**
Smith, George (John Lennon's uncle) **13, 19**
Smith, Mimi (John Lennon's aunt) **13, 19, 34**
Smith, Walter **10, 43, 47**
Spenser, Edmund
Faerie Queene, The (1596) **116**
Spitting Image **208**
Sportique **71**
Stagg, Ben **128, 196**
Star, The (club) **34**
Star Trek **208**
Starr, Maureen **169, 220**
Stephen, John **17, 57, 59, 116**
Stevens, Katy **70**
Stigwood, Robert **127**
'Strawberry Fields Forever' (song) **123**
Sutcliffe, Stuart **23, 26, 29, 57, 164**

T

Take Six **71**
Tamla Motown **47**
Taylor, Alastair **39**
Taylor, Derek **43, 44, 47, 53, 214, 220**
A Cellar Full of Noise **44**
Taylor, Iain **115**
'This Boy' (song) **47**
Times, The (London) **122**
Tolkein, J.R.R.
Lord of the Rings (1954/55) **196**
Topper Man **71**
Town (magazine) **57**
Trecamp Village **71**
Trend, The **127**
Twiggy **120**
Two I's **53**

Vaughan, Frankie **53**
Villeneuve, Justin de **120**
Vincent, Gene **29, 164**
Vollmer, Jürgen **26, 35, 39, 164**
Voormann, Klaus **26, 164, 167, 169, 172**

Watson and Prickard **44**
Waymouth, Nigel **122**
Wikipedia **203**
Williams, Allan **23, 26**
Willis, Bobby **225**
Winterbotham, Neil **214**
Wonderwall (film, 1968) **128**
Wooler, Bob **35, 47**
Wyvern Club (later Blue Angel) **23**

Yellow Submarine (film, 1968) **123**
You And I **71**

Front cover: Photo: K & K Ulf Kruger OHG/Contributor/Getty Images
Back cover: left to right: Details fom pp. 56, 109, 132, 14.

Prestel Verlag, Munich
A member of Verlagsgruppe Random House GmbH

Prestel Verlag
Neumarkter Str. 28
81673 Munich
Tel. +49 (0)89 4136 - 0
Fax +49 (0)89 4136 - 2335

www.prestel.de

Prestel Publishing Ltd.
4 Bloomsbury Place
London WC1A 2QA
Tel. +44 (0)20 7323 - 5004
Fax +44 (0)20 7636 - 8004

Prestel Publishing
900 Broadway, Suite 603
New York, NY 10003
Tel. +1 (212) 995 - 2720
Fax +1 (212) 995 - 2733

www.prestel.com

Library of Congress Control Number: 2011929007

British Library Cataloguing-in-Publication Data: a catalogue record for this book is available from the British Library; Deutsche Nationalbibliothek holds a record of this publication in the Deutsche Nationalbibliografie; detailed bibliographical data can be found under: http://dnb.d-nb.de

Prestel books are available worldwide. Please contact your nearest bookseller or one of the above addresses for information concerning your local distributor.

Editorial direction Philippa Hurd
Editorial assistance and picture research Supriya Malik
Copyediting Matthew Taylor
Production Friederike Schirge
Art direction Cilly Klotz
Design, layout and typesetting SOFAROBOTNIK, Augsburg & Munich
Origination Reproline Genceller, Munich
Printing and Binding Druckerei Uhl GmbH & Co KG, Radolfzell

Printed in Germany

ISBN 978-3-7913-4563-5

Verlagsgruppe Random House FSC®-DEU-0100
The FSC®-certified paper Profisilk had been supplied by Igepa, Germany.